PROMISE AND PERIL

THE McDONALD
CENTER FOR
AMERICA'S FOUNDING
PRINCIPLES

MERCER
UNIVERSITY

The A. V. Elliott Conference Series

The Thomas C. and Ramona E. McDonald Center
for America's Founding Principles

Guided by James Madison's maxim that "a well-instructed people alone
can be permanently a free people," the McDonald Center exists to promote the study of the great texts and ideas that have shaped our regime
and fostered liberal learning.

Directors
Will R. Jordan and Charlotte C. S. Thomas

Published Volumes
Charlotte C. S. Thomas, ed., *No Greater Monster nor Miracle than Myself:
The Political Philosophy of Michel de Montaigne*
Charlotte C. S. Thomas, ed., *Of Sympathy and Selfishness: The Moral and
Political Philosophy of Adam Smith*
Will R. Jordan and Charlotte C. S. Thomas, ed., *The Most Sacred Free-
dom: Religious Liberty in the History of Philosophy and America's Founding*

PROMISE AND PERIL

Republics and Republicanism in the History of Political Philosophy

Edited by Will R. Jordan

MERCER UNIVERSITY PRESS | *Macon, Georgia*

2017

MUP/ P523

© 2017 by Mercer University Press
Published by Mercer University Press
1501 Mercer University Drive
Macon, Georgia 31207
All rights reserved

9 8 7 6 5 4 3 2 1

Books published by Mercer University Press are printed on acid-free
paper that meets the requirements of the American National
Standard for Information Sciences—Permanence of Paper for
Printed Library Materials.

ISBN   978-0-88146-619-5
Cataloging-in-Publication Data is available from the Library of
Congress

CONTENTS

CONTRIBUTORS

Christine Dunn Henderson—Senior Fellow, Liberty Fund Inc., Indianapolis, Indiana

Will R. Jordan—Associate Professor of Political Science, Co-Director of the McDonald Center for America's Founding Principles, Mercer University, Macon, Georgia

Andrea Kowalchuk—Instructor in the Herbst Program in Humanities, University of Colorado, Boulder, Colorado

Michelle A. Schwarze—Postdoctoral Fellow in Political Science, University of Wisconsin, Madison, Wisconsin

Mark Shiffman—Associate Professor of Classical Studies, Villanova University, Villanova, Pennsylvania

Evanthia Speliotis—Professor of Philosophy, Bellarmine University, Louisville, Kentucky

Benjamin Storey—Associate Professor of Political Science, Co-Director of the Tocqueville Program, Furman University, Greenville, South Carolina

Aristide Tessitore—Professor of Political Science, Co-Director of the Tocqueville Program, Furman University, Greenville, South Carolina

Lise van Boxel—Tutor, St. John's College, Santa Fe, New Mexico

James R. Zink—Assistant Professor of Political Science, North Carolina State University, Raleigh, North Carolina

ACKNOWLEDGMENTS

There are a number of people who deserve special recognition for their contributions to this volume. The essays collected here were originally presented at the 2015 A.V. Elliott Conference on Great Books and Ideas, sponsored by Mercer University's Thomas C. and Ramona E. McDonald Center for America's Founding Principles. Neither the Center nor the Conference could deliver their excellent programs without the generosity of the Elliott and McDonald families, and we thank them for this support. The McDonald Center is also fortunate to have strong institutional partners, and I would like to thank Mercer President William D. Underwood, former Provost Wallace Daniel, and successive College of Liberal Arts Deans Lake Lambert and Keith Howard for their efforts to nurture and promote the Center over the years. I especially thank Charlotte Thomas, my co-director at the McDonald Center, for her wonderful leadership and valued friendship as we worked together on this exciting project. This book is as much hers as it is mine.

I am very grateful to Christine Dunn Henderson, Andrea Kowalchuk, Michelle Schwarze, Mark Shiffman, Evanthia Speliotis, Benjamin Storey, Aristide Tessitore, and Lise van Boxel for attending the Elliott Conference and for contributing their essays to this volume. I always marvel at the generosity and professionalism of our visiting scholars, but this group truly set a new standard. I would also like to thank our Mercer undergraduate student panelists who dazzled the conference with their scholarship and poise; so, thank you, Brandon Brock, Jackson Brown, Jazmine Buckley, Maggie Callahan, and Anna Mae Kersey. David Wootton and Stuart Warner are also to be commended for the impressive scholarly contributions they made to the 2015 Elliott Conference.

To prepare for the Elliott Conference, the McDonald Center spent much of the 2014-15 school year considering ancient and modern theories of republicanism. Central to this preparation were two faculty-student reading groups. The groups met weekly to discuss Plutarch's *Lives* and Montesquieu's *Spirit of the Laws*. I am grateful to all of the participants of these reading groups. Each of them made important contributions to our year-long conversation on republicanism. Thank you Charlotte Thomas, Garland Crawford, Kevin Honeycutt, Tom Huber, Kathy Kloepper, Anna Weaver, Tyler Arnold, Matthew Ault, Scott Bradford, Brandon Brock, Jazmine Buckley, Maggie Callahan, Colleen Closson, Abby Hundley, Anna Mae Kersey, Yash Patel, and William Scruggs. I am also grateful to the Apgar Foundation for providing a generous grant that was used to support these reading groups, and to James R. Stoner Jr. for visiting campus and sharing his insights with the Montesquieu group.

Marc Jolley and Mercer University Press have been wonderful to work with on this and every volume in this series. I thank them for catching my mistakes and for giving us, once again, a beautiful book.

Finally, I thank my wife, Anissa, for making possible my work with the Center, and my sons, Evan and Alex—citizens in training.

INTRODUCTION

Will R. Jordan

The essays in this volume were originally prepared for the 2015 A.V. Elliott Conference on Great Books and Ideas at Mercer University. Inspired in part by the landmark work of Paul Rahe,[1] we conceived of the conference as a broad survey of ancient and modern theories of republicanism, with an eye to how they might have influenced the founding of the American republic. Rahe's book identifies a variety of important differences that exist between the civic-minded and tightly-knit republics of the ancient world, and the liberal, individualistic, and commercial republicanism that emerges in the modern era. Our essays largely accept, and in several cases help illuminate, this essential divide. However, what also emerges from these essays is a sense of the timelessness of many of the core dilemmas of popular government, even as the favored solutions may change over time.

How do we balance the pursuit of private interests with the common good? To what extent can leadership and statesmanship be made compatible with the ideas of equality and popular sovereignty? How do we deal with the perennial threat posed by factions, or by the potential for popular passions to overwhelm rational deliberation? What do citizens need to know, and what characteristics must they have, in order to exercise responsibly the power to govern themselves and others? How is the balance to be struck between individual rights and civic duties? To what extent, and under what conditions, is freedom compatible with equality? What do we even mean by freedom? What is the proper relationship between the government and the governed, and how do we prevent republican citizens from becoming mere subjects? All of these questions and dilemmas are, in one way or

---

[1] Paul Rahe, *Republics Ancient and Modern* (Chapel Hill: The University of North Carolina Press, 1992).

another, examined in the pages to follow, though they resist easy and obvious answers.

In addition to revealing the timelessness of these core dilemmas, the essays also share a sense that republicanism, despite its merits and widespread success in the modern world, is forever fragile and fraught with danger. Americans may be familiar with Benjamin Franklin's famous, and perhaps apocryphal, quip following the constitutional convention in 1787, that his fellow delegates had given their countrymen "a republic, if you can keep it." Despite the implicit warning here, there is little doubt that most citizens—and perhaps especially the scholars and pundits who should know better—take our freedoms and form of government for granted most of the time. We appear shocked when we discover that popular government is capable of generating undesirable or even dangerous outcomes.[2] It is for this reason that a volume like this is especially necessary, reminding students and scholars alike that republican government—even one blessed with the careful and seemingly self-regulating institutional mechanisms we find in the U.S. Constitution—has inherent weaknesses as well as strengths. If we are to keep the republic, we must take some care in identifying the points of greatest vulnerability.

---

[2] This introduction was written in the summer of 2016, in the wake of turbulent populist movements in both major U.S. parties during their presidential selection process, as well as the controversial British referendum vote to leave the EU. It is as yet unclear what these events portend for the future of popular government in the West, but they have no doubt led to a great deal of ink being spilled that predicts the worst. See, for example: Adam Gopnik, "The Dangerous Acceptance of Donald Trump," *The New Yorker*, May 20, 2016, retrieved online June 30, 2016; David Frum, "The Seven Broken Guardrails of Democracy," *The Atlantic*, May 31, 2016, retrieved online June 30, 2016; Andrew Sullivan, "Democracies end when they are too democratic: And right now, America is a breeding ground for tyranny," *New York Magazine*, May 1, 2016, retrieved online June 30, 2016; Uri Friedman, "Should the Brexit Vote Have Happened at All," *The Atlantic*, June 27, 2016, retrieved online June 30, 2016; Eric Schnurer, "The End of Democracy as We Know It," *U.S. News and World Report*, June 25, 2016, retrieved online June 30, 2016. There is also a case to be made here that these events may signal a republican pushback against an increasingly distant and unrepresentative administrative state.

The book is divided into three parts. The first part explores two accounts of ancient republicanism; the second surveys several important contributions to republican theory made in the modern era; and the final part focuses on one thinker, Alexis de Tocqueville, and his unique and remarkably prescient contributions to our understanding of modern democratic republics.

The book opens with Evanthia Speliotis' "Regime, Law, and Statesmanship," which provides a close reading of Book III of Aristotle's *Politics*. She explains how the central observations of Aristotle's political science, rooted as they are in the natural capacities of human beings, provide important lessons for republican government. Although Aristotle defines the political community in such a way that naturally lends itself to republicanism—as a community of free human beings who are equally capable of participating in rule through the capacity for reasoned speech—he also recognizes that the common good of that community is constantly threatened by the divisive power of human passions. Speliotis examines how Aristotle recommends treating this problem through the application of the rule of law, political deliberation, and the cultivation of prudential statesmanship. The essay serves as a fitting introduction to the book, as it lays bare Aristotle's remarkable ability to identify the fundamental questions of a topic; we will see these same questions, in one form or another, in many of the subsequent essays.

Mark Shiffman's "Why Publius?" asks why Plutarch selected the life of Publius Valerius Publicola to frame the narrative of the birth of the Roman republic, despite the fact that several other figures appear more likely, even to the point of overshadowing Publius in his own story. Shiffman concludes that Publius is chosen to highlight the "essential predicament of the citizen-statesman in a republic." This predicament emerges because, in order to rule, a potential republican statesman must convince his fellow citizens that he is worthy of rule, possessing extraordinary virtue. He must do this, however, without arousing either his fellow citizens' envy or their suspicion that he harbors excessive personal ambition. Shiffman carefully explains how Plutarch's account of Publius provides a perfect model of how to manage this predicament. Publius' expertise here explains in part why he appears to recede into the background of his own story. Though it exceeds the scope of Shiffman's essay, we might ask whether or not James Madison, Alexander Hamilton, and John Jay had any inkling of this teaching when they selected Publius as their pseudonym when writing the *Federalist Papers*.

Part II opens with the chapter "Montaigne and Modern Republicanism," by Benjamin Storey. While Storey admits that Montaigne seems a strange choice here, given the largely apolitical nature of his work, he makes a compelling case that it is this very quality that makes Montaigne the founder of a new, distinctly modern republicanism that privileges the private sphere over the public. Storey describes how Montaigne's "ateleological, apolitical moral naturalism" serves as an alternative not only to the classical and Christian traditions, but also to another, competing variety of modern republicanism—the "hyper-political, Promethean anti-naturalism" of Niccolo Machiavelli. In describing Montaigne's alternative, Storey identifies four virtues—nonchalance, frankness, authenticity, and humanity—that ennoble the retreat into the private sphere. He also discusses how Montaigne adopts a new attitude toward law and politics that befits his novel moral vision.

Andrea Kowalchuk's "The Foundations of Locke's Defense of Political Toleration and the Limits of Reason," reexamines the writings of one of the chief architects of modern republicanism in light of his curious neglect among those today who have largely followed his lead. Although Locke laid the foundations for the idea of the modern liberal republic, marked by the mutual toleration of free individuals, Kowalchuk contends that contemporary liberals rarely take seriously his arguments for toleration. This is because they seek only a rational, secular, universal defense of toleration, while Locke includes among his reasons a distinctly religious argument, and continues to ground his morality in the existence of a providential God. Kowalchuk takes seriously Locke's reasons for doing so, finding that the religious arguments are made necessary by his conclusions about the limits of human reason. She argues that Locke's epistemology casts real doubt on the very possibility of a rational, secular, universal defense of toleration. Ultimately, she suggests, Locke's religiously grounded argument might prove more universal, and more tolerant, than the contemporary theories that seek to supplant him.

In their "Reconciling Natural Rights and the Moral Sense in Francis Hutcheson's Republicanism," Michelle Schwarze and James Zink correct what they see as a fundamental error in Hutcheson scholarship. In recent decades, critics of a hyper-individualistic, Lockean strand of modern republicanism have turned to Francis Hutcheson's moral philosophy, and especially to his doctrines of an inherent moral sense and universal benevolence, to provide a communitarian alternative. Schwarze and Zink argue that these critics ignore the fact that Hutcheson's *political* philosophy in fact largely follows the Lockean framework of limited government and natural rights. Instead of ignoring this seeming paradox, Schwarze and Zink seek to reconcile Hutcheson's moral and political thought. They do so by showing that Hutcheson consistently understood the moral sense and benevolence to be fully compatible with innocent forms of self-interest and self-love (and therefore did not see private interest and public duties as mutually exclusive categories), and that Hutcheson's prescriptions for limited government follow from his general worries about the limits of human understanding when it comes to both our analytical and moral reasoning. In this sense, the chapter pairs nicely with Kowalchuk's in showing the importance of skeptical epistemology in the rise of modern republicanism.

The book's final part examines the writings and thought of Alexis de Tocqueville. Lise van Boxel's "Tocqueville's New Science of Politics" works through how Tocqueville conceived of the need for a new political science in an increasingly democratic age. The novel problem to be solved here, according to van Boxel, is how to reconcile freedom and equality while preserving both. Especially vulnerable here is freedom—the republican freedom of governing oneself and participating in politics—when it is threatened by the individual impotence and envy that come with the creeping equality of conditions. Van Boxel describes Tocqueville's chief worry of a new, soft despotism emerging in the modern world, a despotism capable of degrading human beings below the level of humanity. She also articulates his solutions, including the need for vibrant civil associations and healthy religious life. The chapter ends, however, by questioning whether Tocqueville's solutions go far enough in committing his new science to the ultimate task of fostering human greatness. Her Tocqueville seems at least one step short of accomplishing his full aims.

Christine Dunn Henderson's "Tocqueville on Modern Individualism" focuses a bit more narrowly on Tocqueville's ambivalence about the rise of individualism that comes with modern democracy. She explains how an excessive concern with self and retreat from the public sphere follow naturally from democracy, and shares Tocqueville's fears that these inevitable trends make us ever more vulnerable to the threats of majority tyranny and soft despotism. In describing Tocqueville's solutions, she treats explicitly a key issue that emerges at several points in this volume. Tocqueville does not think it possible to do away with the individualism and self-interest that emerge with modern democracy. As a result, he does not try to replace self-interest with a return to ancient patriotism or self-sacrifice. Instead, he uses free institutions and civil associations to remind citizens that their own interests overlap at many points with those around them. Instead of selflessness, it is self-interest well understood that can serve as the glue that binds the modern republic.

The book ends with Aristide Tessitore's "Alexis de Tocqueville and Abraham Lincoln on Modern Republicanism." He points out that these two near contemporaries shared a common concern that the American political order required more than the institutional scaffolding provided by the Constitution, both fearing that it did not "articulate a deep shared purpose that might hold America together at a moment of grave internal crisis." Interestingly, they turned to a different foundation to remedy this problem: Lincoln to the natural rights principles of the Declaration of Independence, and Tocqueville to the Christianity of the Puritan forebears. In comparing these solutions, Tessitore examines the relative advantages of abstract philosophic principles and religious mores, concluding that both Lincoln and Tocqueville understood what was at stake in the choice, and in fact may be closer to each other than they first appear. No matter the choice, the chapter reminds us once again of the limits inherent in politics, and that the future of freedom is not inevitable; it requires both careful study and prudential statesmanship.

In the end, we hope that this volume will be useful to both citizens and scholars. The essays all take seriously the task of identifying and responding to the dilemmas inherent in republican politics. They remind us of both the promise and perils in our great political experiment, and of the always unfinished work involved in keeping a republic.

PART I

ON ANCIENT REPUBLICANISM

I

REGIME, LAW, AND STATESMANSHIP

Evanthia Speliotis

The founding of the American regime, in particular as expressed and instantiated in the U.S. Constitution, is a striking example of political theory in action. While some of this theory arose from the founders' reflections on the lessons of history, some of it is traceable to philosophical discussions that began in antiquity in the writings of Plato, Aristotle, and Cicero. For example, the regime structure that is embodied in the U.S. Constitution resonates with and is reflective of the writings of Aristotle and Cicero on the form and structure of the best regime. Likewise, the importance and centrality of the rule of law for truly just—i.e., non-tyrannical—rule embraced by the founders appears to be a direct application of the arguments presented by both Plato and Aristotle about why, though law can only provide general rules rather than the precise prescriptions that a wise ruler could supply, the rule of law must nevertheless be paramount and the supreme office of the land. Finally, though the establishment of an independent judiciary—in the body of the Supreme Court—is distinctly modern and novel, several of the arguments adduced in support of such a body reflect arguments presented by both Plato and Aristotle regarding the need for prudential (*phronimos*) statesmanship to supplement the general prescriptions of the law in order to ensure that justice will truly be done.

For the purposes of this essay, I wish to examine Aristotle's discussion of three questions in particular from the *Politics*, which, I believe, contribute substantially to understanding the experiment that we know as the U.S. Constitution. Those questions are (a) what, according to Aristotle, constitutes a regime (*politeia*) and how ought it be structured; (b) what is the importance and proper place of law in a good regime; and (c) what is the nature and role of statesmanship (*politike*), the particular kind of knowledge necessary for wise and just rule.

To begin, a brief note about translation. The Greek word that I am rendering as "regime" is "*politeia*." "*Politeia*" both in form and in the way that Aristotle employs it in his discussion implies the form (in the Platonic sense) or definition of what it is to be the structured unity that is truly a political community. While I prefer the word "regime" to translate "*politeia*," an equally good translation would be "constitution," insofar as "constitution," like "regime," also points to the structured whole. Another translation that is fairly popular for "*politeia*," and which can be traced back to Cicero as the Latin term he proffers, though it is somewhat removed from the idea of form or structure, is "republic."[1]

The Political Community

Aristotle opens the discussion of the *Politics* by insisting that the political community or association (*koinonia*) is a unique kind of community.[2] With this, he is setting himself in opposition to a claim made in Plato's *Statesman*, which suggests that different sorts of community—political, kingly, household, and master-slave—differ only in size, not in kind, and for this reason, that the nature of rule is essentially the same for all.[3] Beginning in this way, Aristotle sets the stage to discuss, first, what is the unique nature of the political com-

---

[1] The work we English speakers know as Plato's *Republic* has as its Greek title *Politeia*, following Cicero, who declared that the political community or the state is "the people's affair" (*res publica*). Cicero, *On the Commonwealth*, trans. George Holland Sabine and Stanley Barney Smith (Indianapolis, IN: Bobbs-Merrill Educational Publishing, 1976) xxv.

[2] All subsequent references to the *Politics* can be found in Aristotle, *The Politics*, trans. Carnes Lord (Chicago, IL: Chicago University Press, 1984).

[3] *Statesman* 259b. Although, as the argument of the *Statesman* unfolds, this supposed identification is undercut. At the very least, by the middle of the *Statesman*, the Eleatic Stranger has decisively distinguished between statesmanship and slave-mastery (see *Statesman* 276d11-e12). Plato, *The Statesman*, trans. Seth Benardete (Chicago, IL: University of Chicago Press, 1984).

munity that sets it apart from other kinds of community, and, second, what is the proper nature of rule that is uniquely fitting and appropriate to a *political* community per se.[4]

The first thing that Aristotle distinguishes that makes the political community unique is its end (aim, goal: *telos*). Every association, he declares, is constituted for the sake of some end (1252a1-3). The end of slave-mastery is some good or goal of the master for whom the slave is a tool (1254a14-17; see also 1278b35-37); the end of a household is to satisfy "daily needs" (1252b13; see also 1278b37-40); the end of a kingship is the virtue or excellence of the subjects (1259a41). Standing apart, the end of the political association, according to Aristotle, is "living well" (*eu zein*: 1252b30), a phrase we know from the *Nicomachean Ethics* to be associated with virtue, happiness, and the good life.[5] Beginning his discussion of "the political things" as he does with reference to happiness and virtue would seem to set Aristotle at some distance from modern and contemporary understandings of politics, which are skeptical, if not outright dismissive, of the talk of "ends" and "virtue" that are implicit in "living well."[6] The end or goal

---

[4] See Locke, *Second Treatise of Government*, ed. C. B. Macpherson (Indianapolis, IN: Hackett Publishing Company, Inc., 1980) chap. 1, sec. 2: "that the power of a *magistrate* over a subject may be distinguished from that of a *father* over his children, a *master* over his servant, a *husband* over his wife, and a *lord* over his slave."

[5] This phrase is reminiscent of the *Nicomachean Ethics*, with its extensive discussion of virtue (*arête*: excellence, happiness, and living well). Early in his discussion in the *Ethics*, Aristotle says that "the many and the educated (*oi charientes*) identify the final, highest end of human life as happiness (*eudaimonia*) and understand by this 'living well' and 'faring well' (*eu zein, eu prattein*)" (1095a18-20). The remainder of the *Nicomachean Ethics* may be understood as Aristotle's investigation into what this means. And yet, even the *Ethics*' discussion does not seem to suffice since, at the end, Aristotle says that it is necessary to examine "legislation (*nomthesia*) and the whole problem of the structure of the regime (*peri politeias*) in order to bring to completion as much as possible the philosophy of the human things" (1181b13-15). Aristotle, *Nicomachean Ethics*, trans. Martin Ostwald (Englewood Cliffs, NJ: Prentice Hall, 1962).

[6] See, for example, Hobbes, *Leviathan*, ed. C. B. Macpherson (New York, NY: Penguin Books, 1968) part I, chap. 11: "For there is no such *Finis ultimus*,

of the political association, however, is not some arbitrary or even abstractly idealistic goal pulled down from the heavens. Rather, it is rooted in and derived from the nature and capacities of the constituent members of the association. And it is this point—that it is the nature and capacities of human beings that are the proper foundation and origin of the political community—and everything that it entails, such as the kind of rule that is fitting for beings with such capacities as human beings have, that finds deep resonance in modernity, up to and including the discussions among the founders of the American republic.

Thus, besides having the particular end in common of living well, what makes a political community unique and distinct from other communities is that it is a community of free and equal human beings (*Politics* 1252a1-4; 1255b20). "Freedom" in this definition designates not a political or nominal identification, but a capacity that belongs to human beings by their very nature. To be free in principle or by nature is to have the capacity to reason and speak (*"logos echein"*). Having this capacity means one is able to entertain opinions and engage in conversations about the good and bad and the just and unjust (1253a10-19), to develop one's understanding through these conversations, and therefore to be able to rule oneself: to be author and authority over one's own actions. Having this capacity qualifies one to participate in one's own rule, i.e., to participate in decision (*krisis*) and office (*arche*) (1275a23), deliberation and judgment (1275b18-19).[7] The alternative to being free is either to be a slave or to be a child. A child is potentially free and simply needs the education and guidance to develop his reason to the point where he can rule himself; a slave— i.e., someone who is by nature a slave and has no potential to be free—according to Aristotle, lacks any capacity, whether in the pre-

---

(utmost ayme,) nor *Summum Bonum,* (greatest Good,) as is spoken of in the Books of the old Morall Philosophers."

[7] See Locke, *Second Treatise,* chap. 6: "we are born *free,* as we are born rational" (sec. 61); "the *freedom* then of man, and liberty of acting according to his own will, is *grounded on* his having *reason*" (sec. 63).

sent or future, to rule himself.[8] Anyone who is by nature free—i.e., who has the capacity to think and to exercise authority over himself— qualifies to participate in rule; to preclude such an individual from having some share in rule is, according to Aristotle, unjust.[9]

Having identified the nature of the constituents of the political community, and the proper end, the challenge that Aristotle turns to address is how best to order and structure this collectivity of free and equal individuals so as to weave them together into a unified whole— a true community—that acknowledges and respects their capacities, on the one hand, and that allows and even enables them to work toward achieving the end, on the other. As he turns to address this question, there is, however, an additional difficulty he must address: the "free and equal" individuals who are entitled to have a share in the political community—to be called "citizens" and to participate in deliberation and judgment and, thereby, in their own self-rule (1275b18-20)—are not, from the outset, wise.[10] Lacking wisdom, they tend to be driven, and ruled, by their passions and (private) in-

---

[8] Though the received opinion about Aristotle is that Aristotle is arguing for natural slavery, the conditions he outlines that would justify calling someone "slave" suggest that only a being that is not human, a being that has no speech or reason or reasoning ability whatsoever could possibly qualify. See, for example, Book I, chap. 5, where Aristotle defines a "slave by nature" as one who "stands apart from other human beings as much as the soul [differs] from the body or as a human being, from a beast" (1254b16-19). Such a one qualifies as a "possession" (1254a14-17). But, by Aristotle's very definition, "slave by nature" appears to be a category with no members.

[9] See Locke's assertion that, in the state of nature, all men are perfectly free to rule themselves. Locke, *Second Treatise of Government*, chap. II, sec. 4.

[10] It is Plato, not Aristotle, who states this point directly. In the *Statesman*, where Plato is grappling with the question of who should rule and what is the best form of regime, he recognizes that "there is no king who comes-to-be in the cities...who is of the sort that naturally arises in beehives—one who is right from the start exceptional in his body and soul..." (*Stsm* 301d-e). The *Nicomachean Ethics*, however, may be understood as one long discussion about what human beings need to do to move from their natural ignorance toward wisdom. And the argument of the *Politics*, as we shall see, proceeds on the understanding that human beings are not wise by nature (birth).

terests, which they express as opinions. These opinions they then strive to impose on everyone. As is so often the case when opinions and not knowledge reign supreme, one individual's or group's opinions will be in conflict with others'. For as each individual and group ardently promotes its own, narrowly conceived private self-interest, it tends to ignore the good of the community or the whole. Insofar as every actual community of human beings will have groups (factions) with various and competing interests, the result will be constant bickering and strife, which may escalate to the point of civil war or even revolution.[11] In such a situation, the prevailing party or faction will impose its limited (or partial) understanding of justice on everyone, ignoring the legitimate competing interests and claims of other parties or factions. Might will make right, and justice will never be achieved. This absence of wisdom, which is a fact of human life and of the human condition, is a threat to the existence and preservation of the state and to any possibility of justice, and must be addressed if one is to have any hope of achieving justice.[12]

To illustrate this point, Aristotle turns to consider the two particular, competing opinions that seem to arise repeatedly across regime types and across time: they are the claims and understandings of the rich, on the one hand, and of the poor, on the other, or, in the language of Aristotle's day, the interests of the relatively few landed gentry, otherwise known as the aristocrats or oligarchs, *versus* the interests of the many commoners, i.e., non-aristocrats, or plebeians

---

[11] See *Federalist* 10: "By a faction I understand a number of citizens … who are united and actuated by some common impulse of passion, or of interest, adverse to the rights of other citizens, or to the permanent and aggregate interests of the community"; and "As long as the reason of man continues fallible, and he is at liberty to exercise it, different opinions will be formed." *The Federalist Papers*, ed. Clinton Rossiter (New York, NY: Penguin Group, 1961) 78.

[12] See *Pol* 1279a17-21: "those regimes which look to the common advantage are correct regimes according to what is unqualifiedly just, while those which look only to the advantage of the rulers are errant, and are all deviations from the correct regime; for they involve mastery, but the city is a partnership of free persons."

(1280a7 ff.).[13] The gentry, who are wealthy, understand the good to be wealth and claim that they have the right to rule by virtue of having wealth. For, having wealth, they have a certain virtue (excellence) that others (the poor) lack, and because of this virtue they stand apart. Being unequal (i.e., superior in wealth) they claim to deserve unequal merit (i.e., superiority in political power). The many and poor, on the other hand, while they do not have (much) property and therefore cannot claim to have a stake in the regime on account of property nevertheless also claim to have a good that deserves acknowledgment and that affords them the right to participate in rule. That good is freedom (*Politics* 1280a23; Cicero's *Commonwealth* xxvii; xxxv), the capacity to think for and therefore to rule themselves.[14] The problem is that each group, according to Aristotle, "fastens on a certain sort of justice, but proceeds only to a certain point and does not speak of the whole of justice in its authoritative sense" (1280a9-11). In other words, people tend to aggrandize their own interests and claims and to minimize others'; this leads them to mistake what is a part of justice for the whole (1280b21). "For the ones, if they are unequal in a certain thing, such as goods, suppose they are unequal generally,

---

[13] See *Federalist* 10: "the most common and durable source of factions has been the various and unequal distributions of property. Those who hold and those who are without property have ever formed distinct interests in society" (79). As for associating the wealthy with the rule of a few (oligarchy) and the poor with the rule of the many, the people (democracy), Aristotle makes it clear that what has implications for the kind of regime is not how many rulers there are, but rather what principle or criterion ("good") they define as the defining principle and end of the regime. It is more appropriate, therefore, to speak of the goods of "wealth" and "freedom" as possible relevant and defining regime principles rather than of the number of rulers (see *Pol* 1279b34-1280a4; see also Plato, *Stsm* 291d-292c). Having made this point, Aristotle nevertheless employs the term "oligarchy" to refer to the rule of the wealthy, and the term "democracy" to refer to the rule of the poor, perhaps on the grounds that in general, the wealthy tend to be few(er) and the poor, many.

[14] Aristotle includes the well born in his list of those who have a legitimate claim to deserve some share in rule, in part, it seems, as a stand-in for virtue (*Pol* 1283a17; 1283a35-38, 38-40). But by far the greater part of his discussion focuses on the competing claims of the rich and the poor.

while the others suppose that if they are equal in a certain thing, such as freedom, they are equal generally" (1280a22-24). Since human beings have a tendency to promote their own (private) interests over the common interest, a pure oligarchy/aristocracy would promote the interest of wealth (or birth) above all others, while a pure democracy would promote the interest of freedom.

And yet, both groups' claims have some merit, according to Aristotle. The wealthy deserve a share in political honors and rule because they own property and, as such, he says, will be "more trustworthy regarding agreements" (1283a33), presumably because they need the protection that the political community affords. And, he claims, "the many, of whom none is individually an excellent man, nevertheless can, when joined together, be better—not as individuals but all together—than those [who are best], just as dinners contributed to [by many] can be better than those equipped from a single expenditure. For because they are many, each can have a part of virtue and prudence" (1281a43-1281b5). Aristotle reiterates this point later when he says, "the majority [has a just claim] in relation to a minority for they are superior and wealthier and better when the majority is taken together in relation to the minority" (1283a40-43).[15] Since both wealth and freedom constitute a partially justified claim, according to Aristotle both groups (interests) deserve a share in rule (office). A truly just regime, therefore, must make room for both.[16]

What neither group recognizes, however, is that for justice to truly be a possibility the community must be united and a one (*hen*), and that means that each (part) must look beyond its partial, partisan interests toward a common advantage or public good ("*koinon sumph-*

---

[15] See *The Anti-Federalist Papers and the Constitutional Convention Debates*, ed. Ralph Ketcham (New York, NY: Penguin Group, 1986) "Qualifications for Suffrage," Aug. 7, 1787, 145-48.

[16] As Cicero says, "In a government dominated by an aristocracy the mass of the people have hardly any share in freedom, since they have no part in common deliberative and executive powers. And when the state is governed by the people, even if they be just and self-disciplined, yet their very equality is inequitable in that it does not recognize degrees of merit" (*On the Commonwealth*, xxvii).

eron": Politics 1279a30; see also Cicero, *Commonwealth*, xxv).[17] For, only "those regimes which look to the common advantage are correct regimes according to what is unqualifiedly just, while those which look only to the advantage of the rulers are errant, and are all deviations from the correct regimes, for they involve mastery" (1279a17-20). The difficulty is that, while Aristotle has identified the true and best end of the political community as "living well," he recognizes what a high degree of wisdom and intelligence the correct identification and understanding of this end requires, and that this understanding may well be absent from a particular community. He allows, therefore, that a given regime might be considered a legitimate regime (though not the best) if it at least has some understanding of a "common advantage" or "public good" as its end, understanding "common advantage" in contrast with private interest or advantage (1279a31-32).[18] At the most minimal, this common advantage is the survival of the community (1278b19-30). Since constant strife threatens the security and stability of the community,[19] the first and necessary goal of the political community must be peace, freedom from strife. Only after this has been secured will the political community be in a position to work toward and discover—presumably through discussions among the citizens (see 1253a18)—what "living well" in its full and complete sense might mean and entail.

What Aristotle has articulated up to this point is the proper end of the political community—both as a practical, minimal necessity (peace and stability) and as a fully actualized ideal (living well). In discussing this he has focused on the nature of the citizens, the differ-

---

[17] The U.S. Constitution is a regime-founding document in this classical sense. Coming in the aftermath of the failed Articles of Confederation, it deliberately set forth to create a united nation that would indeed function as and would be a whole: "a more perfect union." See also Locke, *Second Treatise of Government*, chap. 1, sec. 3: political power is for the sake of "the public good."

[18] Thus, unlike the uniformity that Plato seems to propose in the city in speech in the *Republic*, Aristotle seeks to acknowledge and respect private interests, but he insists that above (or besides) these, there must also be a good that is of the whole.

[19] See Plato's *Statesman* 302a-b.

ent prerogatives that deserve political voice and political recognition, and the very real threat that factionalism—which stems from ignorance and passions—poses to the existence and well-being of the state. Additionally, Aristotle appears to recognize that the absence of wisdom about complete justice and the good eludes a simple solution. The question is, how to achieve the unity that will bring the various competing interests together and into a whole? To override the multiplicity of opinions and achieve unity with force would be unjust. For the rule of force is more akin to tyranny and despotism (slave-mastery) than to political rule insofar as it ignores, and even tramples, the innate freedom of the citizens (subjects). Aristotle briefly considers whether "offices should be unequally distributed in accordance with a pre-eminence in a particular good" (1282b24), but the problem this raises is which good is so significant that it merits a pre-eminence of political power? He wonders in particular whether wealth or good birth should give one a higher prerogative to rule than lack of wealth or lesser birth. His answer, however, is no. For however much of a claim to rule is represented by the wealthy, it is not so significant as to negate entirely the claim made by a non-propertied individual who is rational and therefore free. In fact, Aristotle concludes, "none of the defining principles on the basis of which they [different individuals and groups] claim they merit to rule and all the others merit to be ruled by them is correct" (1283b27-29), and each group's claims "involves difficulties" (1281a15). As a solution to this impasse, Aristotle proposes and turns to examine a different alternative altogether: he proposes that what should be pre-eminent and the most authoritative power in the city is law.

The Rule of Law

At first glance, making law the pre-eminent power in the state appears to substantiate and endorse the democrats' claim to rule above the claims of the wealthy or the well born. For since law is impartiality, that means that under the law, everyone is equal, and, besides claiming freedom as their prerogative and title to rule, the democrats also claim that because they are free they are equal to everyone else (1280a24).[20] But the immediate purpose behind proposing that law be authoritative above all is that law solves the seemingly unavoidable partiality that human beings, no matter who they are, bring to rule. For law stands apart from partiality and blind preference. Law, Aristotle says, "is the mean [*to meson*]" (1287b4); it is "reason without appetite" (1287a33); "one who asks law to rule … is held to be asking god and intellect alone to rule, while one who asks man adds the beast" (1287a28-30). Human passions threaten to undermine the judgments of reason, even in the most virtuous individuals. Laws are general prescriptions that are written down and are intended to apply across time, across persons, and across situations. Being general and impartial, the pronouncements of law are distributive; they apply equally to all. Being written down rather than determined in the immediacy of a situation, they stand above the fray and can be "objective."

There are, however, two problems with law that Aristotle needs to address before he can arrive at the above conclusions. One problem has to do with its origins, the other with its application. Both problems concern knowledge. Let us consider first origins. To introduce the possibility that law should be the authoritative element, Aristotle says, "One might perhaps assert that it is bad for the authoritative element generally to be man instead of law, at least if he has the passions that result from being human in his soul" (1281a34-35). Immediately, however, he raises an objection. If the law is made by oligarchs for oligarchic interests or by democrats for democratic interests, it will be neither impartial nor fair and, indeed, will be no different than if oligarchs or democrats ruled exclusive of the other (1281a36-38). That is to say, why is law not simply the setting in stone of the prejudice and partiality of whoever the ruling party or strongest voice happens to be? What we might expect Aristotle to say here, though he does not, is that law, properly speaking, is to be writ-

---

[20] See also *The Republic of Plato*, ed. Allan Bloom (New York, NY: Basic Books Publishers, 1968) 557a ff.; 558c; 561c; 561e.

ten by a wise statesman, one who has the knowledge and expertise of the art of legislation, akin to the experts in the science of medicine who write the medical textbooks.[21] Such a possibility is considered in the *Statesman* by Plato who, in his discussion about law, first introduces law as analogous to the prescriptions that a knowledgeable doctor might set down in writing if he had to go away for some time. These writings would embody the doctor's knowledge; being written down, they would serve as reflections and reminders of his wisdom in his absence (*Statesman* 295c). By the end of his discussion about law, however, Plato has shifted his focus to the fact that no human being is born with the wisdom of the art of legislation and that laws must be written down for the survival and well-being of the community prior to any such wisdom having been attained by anyone (if it even could be). What this means, Plato concludes, is that what any community of human beings must do in the absence of such wisdom is to set down in writing the best laws possible, and then "run after the traces of the best regime" (*Statesman* 301d-e). As Aristotle turns to address the possibility of law as the highest office, he appears to begin where Plato ends: seemingly accepting Plato's conclusion about the lack of wisdom, he turns to examine how good—i.e., non-partisan and just—laws might come-to-be. And for this, he turns, once more, to the people (*demos*), the many.

Aristotle claims, "The many, of whom none is individually an excellent man, nevertheless can, when joined together, be better—not as individuals but all together—than those who are best" (1281a43-1281b1). He continues, "For because they are many, each can have a part of virtue and prudence, and on their joining together, the multitude, with its many feet and hands and having many senses, becomes like a single human being" (1281b4-7). Aristotle's thought here seems to be (echoing Plato from the *Republic*) that, among the many—the

---

[21] In the *Nicomachean Ethics*, Aristotle claimed that the art of legislation (*nomothetike*) is to the state what practical wisdom (*phronesis*)—the knowledge necessary for virtuous action and hitting the mean—is to the individual (1141b 24-27).

people—one will find expression of all possible views.[22] If you bring all the people together and give them voice, you will have all the possibilities, including the best, available for consideration. To illustrate, Aristotle offers the following analogy: that "dinners contributed to by many can be better equipped than those from a single expenditure" (1281b1-3). At first glance, if this is what giving voice to the people will mean, it seems to be a false claim that what results from them will be better than what would come from "those who are best." Consider, for example, the terribly mismatched and unbalanced selection of foods one might encounter at a pot luck supper, in contrast with the elegance and excellence within each course and across all courses of a gourmet meal. And yet, Aristotle's point seems to be that no one begins as a gourmet chef. Even the gourmet chef had to develop his art through a great deal of experience and across time, perhaps even by experiencing multiple pot luck suppers. The question is, how does one progress from chance-met, ill-formed experience and opinions to wisdom and artfulness?

What is needed, once the various views have been gathered together, is thoughtful consideration and debate. Aristotle reiterates at this point that the many should be allowed to participate in "deliberation and judgment" (1281b31).[23] This is because, as he has already argued, since the many are rational and free (even though not wise), in principle they must have some share in ruling. More pragmatically, if they are not allowed a share in ruling, this poses a danger to the state, as they may revolt (1281b30). But the key point here is "deliberation." If we consider "deliberating" in conjunction with the dinner example, Aristotle's discussion seems to indicate the kind of discussion that a regime should engage in before enacting a particular law. He is not speaking of untutored cooks bringing some canned dish to the dinner. If he were, he would be advocating for a pure, direct de-

---

[22] Plato calls democracy "the most beautiful of regimes ... just like a many-colored (*poikilos*) cloak" (*Republic* 557c).

[23] Although he cautions that they should not "have a share in the greatest offices" because it "is not safe" (1281b26). We will have to return to the question of what these "greatest offices" might be.

mocracy, where everything is determined by direct vote.[24] Instead, Aristotle seems to have in mind that everyone will bring their ideas—shaped by their respective passions, to be sure, but also by their different experiences—to the table and then will participate in discussing and debating those ideas. In this discussion, everyone should be invited to offer his view (contribution), and then to discuss the respective merits and demerits of each of the views. Giving a voice to everyone allows everyone a chance to participate in rule; putting these voices together into a discussion allows for a weighing and a sifting through of the various ideas. The hope is that, by going through this process, the end result (a particular law) will indeed reflect the best thinking of the populace and that this best thinking will be better than any single view proposed before the discussion. Of course for this truly to work, there must indeed be genuine discussion, a true putting to work of the highest possibility that is available to human beings, which is the capacity and opportunity to discuss "the just and the unjust, and other things of this sort" (1253a16).

Statesmanship and Law

Even if good laws can be drafted through this process of deliberation and judgment, however, there still remains a significant problem. The problem with law is that it "speaks only of the universal and [does] not command with a view to circumstance" (1286a11). And yet the application of law is always to a particular situation and circumstance. Precisely because laws are general pronouncements that are written down and are meant to apply across time, persons, and situations, law can never articulate the precise mean (*meson*) required in a given situation.[25] As Aristotle points out, in the arts and sciences—for exam-

---

[24] See *Federalist* 10: "a pure democracy ... can admit of no cure for the mischiefs of faction. A common passion or interest will, in almost every case, be felt by a majority of the whole ... and there is nothing to check the inducements to sacrifice the weaker party or an obnoxious individual" (81).

[25] Plato's *Statesman* gives, perhaps, the best articulation of this difficulty: "a law would never be capable of comprehending with precision for all simultaneously the best and the most just, and enjoining the best.... It is impossible, then,

ple, in medicine—"to rule in accordance with written [rules] is fool-ish" (1286a13). If the health of the patient truly is going to be achieved, it will require more than just the science of medicine out-lined in the medical books. It will require someone knowledgeable—a doctor—to weigh the particularities of the situation as well. No good (i.e., knowledgeable, virtuous) doctor is simply or blindly going to follow the science of medicine outlined in the medical books. He is going to look at the particulars of the patient before him, and then is going to tailor the medical book's prescriptions so that they fit this particular case.[26] Similarly, Aristotle is claiming, what law lacks and is in need of if justice is to be met is a similar knowledge, which Aristo-tle calls prudence or practical wisdom ("*phronesis*"), of how to hit the mean in a particular set of circumstances. A prudential judgment can-not be legislated. As deliberation and judgment are necessary for the crafting of good laws, so too deliberation and judgment are necessary for the just execution of those laws. The just execution of laws re-quires a prudential statesman: someone—or a few someones—who plays a role in political matters analogous to the role of the doctor in medical matters.

At this point, someone might wonder whether, if laws are inad-equate to address the particularity inherent in every situation, and if a prudential statesman will know more precisely and better than the

---

for that which is simple through all times [namely, law] to be in a good condition relative to things that are never simple [namely, human beings and the situations in which they find themselves]" (294a-c).

[26] See also Plato's *Statesman* 295c-e, where he offers the following scenario. Suppose a doctor is going away for a while and writes down prescriptions (laws) for his patients to follow while he is away. When the doctor returns, the doctor will be able to prescribe something more accurate and precise than what he had previously written down. Surely, Plato says, the doctor would not confine himself to those previous writings, but would instead bring his knowledge to bear on the situation and would prescribe what his science indicated even if it ran counter to the law. For law is general, whereas "the dissimilarities of human beings and of their actions and the fact that almost none of the human things is ever at rest do not allow any art whatsoever to declare in any case anything simple about all and over the entire time" (294a-b).

laws what the just prescription is in a given situation, should not the prudential statesman be the supreme authority in the state? For if someone is truly artful, truly knowledgeable, laws will be an impediment. At the very least, because laws are general, the prudent statesman will always know better and more precisely than any law what should be done. Even worse, because they arose from a committee, a collectivity of not wise individuals, a given set of laws might not even be the best pronouncements possible (even at a general level). Aristotle therefore considers the possibility that, if there should be someone in a state who has this level of wisdom—and "prudence" means knowledge of both the good, i.e., the universal principle, and knowledge of the best application of that good to the circumstances—that person does not need law and should rule simply. He calls this individual "*pambasileus*": an absolute king, authoritative over all (1284b27-34).

In the end, however, the *pambasileus* is not an answer for Aristotle. For one thing, even if there were such a supremely wise and virtuous individual, if he ruled absolutely, he would reduce the city to a household as he would know better than everyone what was best to do, which in turn would reduce everyone simply to following and obeying his commands.[27] But this is not a political arrangement, and it violates the principle that those who are by nature free justly deserve to have some share in their own self-governance. Furthermore, Aristotle appears to be deeply skeptical that such a wise individual could ever be found. For one thing, being a human being, he is in danger of being susceptible to the weakness that besets human beings when it comes to judgment and rule, and that is that they will be led not by their intellect but by their desires and appetites. And it is at this point that Aristotle says, "one who asks law to rule is held to be

[27] See *Politics* 1285b30-34. Aristotle introduces the *pambasileus* as akin to a household manager, saying: the kind of kingship "when one person has authority over all matters … [is] an arrangement that resembles household management. For just as rule of the household manager is a kind of kingship over the house, so [this kind of] kingship is household management for a city or a nation."

asking god and intellect alone to rule; one who asks man to rule adds the beast" (1287a30).

Let us therefore return to consider law once more. Aristotle's account would be strange and unsatisfying if he were advocating the simple (and very possibly ignorant and unjust) decision by compromise that may occur when a collectivity of individuals comes to the table armed only with their preferences and private interests, and were allowing that this be the highest office in the state. This, however, does not appear to be what he is doing. For one thing, he only supports as authoritative those laws that are "correctly enacted," which means, those laws "that are enacted with a view to the regime" (1282b10). The best regime is one that gives a place and a voice to everyone who has a legitimate claim to participate in rule, that is, everyone who has reason. But not only do the poor have a share in reason, the wealthy do as well. The crafting of laws therefore should draw from all parts and constituents of the state. Absent wisdom, Aristotle privileges tradition and custom: the lessons accrued over much experience and time, and the decisions that have withstood the test of time (1287b4). But he is not advocating that we be hidebound to our customs and traditions. Always and at every level there must be deliberation and judgment. That means that always there must be room for the possibility of discovering something better, and enacting it: replacing what was decided before that has now been discovered to be incorrect (1287a27).

There is, however, yet one more layer to what Aristotle understands by "law." On the one hand, he clearly seems to be speaking about the legislation that governs the daily lives of citizens, arguing that this must be the job of legislators who come from all parts of the community and who represent all of the various interests and voices in the community. On the other hand, "law" also points beyond such particular legislation, to the very structure of the regime itself. This is the law that articulates the order and structure of the regime—the distribution and assignment of the offices (*archai*). Every other function within the regime is subordinate to law in this sense, as Aristotle underlines every time he insists that what is just in a given regime is what is in keeping with the nature and principles of that regime. That means that every level of governance by human beings must be subordinate to law as the arrangement of offices. And the arrangement of offices, and the qualifications for each office, delineate "the arrangement of ruling and being ruled in turn" (1287a18). This is law as constitution.

Understanding law as constitution—i.e., reflecting and embodying the defining principles of the regime—the role of everyone within the regime is to enact those principles as "law-guardians and servants of the law" (1287a23). That is to say, it is the job of each to do the task for which he is qualified when it comes to be his turn to rule. The constitutional apportionment of tasks and power in Aristotle's account is political.[28] There is the office of legislator, and this office will be open to the largest part of the citizenry (the many), who have the capacity for and therefore deserve to have a voice in "deliberation and judgment." As Aristotle seems to make clear, the many must be given a voice and power with regard to the drafting of legislation (the kind of legislation that governs daily life) for all the reasons discussed earlier. The executive function of the state—namely, the rulers[29]—which requires, as far as possible, prudential judgment, and a proper fitting of the principles of law to the particular situations at hand, will be open to individuals of greater experience and wisdom.[30] As Aristotle notes, it is law itself that "hands over what remains undetermined [by law itself] to be judged and administered 'by the most just decision' of the rulers" (1287a26). Part of this as well would seem to include the judicial function of adjudicating transgressions of the law.

---

[28] That is to say, in *Politics* Book III. *Politics* Book IV turns to discuss the composition of the city more in terms of functional tasks like farmer, merchant, etc. (see *Pol* 1290b40 ff.).

[29] *Politics* 1287b8 ff. This is what Aristotle seemed to mean earlier when he said the many were not fit for the "highest offices."

[30] Ideally, these would be the most virtuous (see *Politics* 1281a4-8; 1283a20-21) but how to gauge virtue seems to be an insurmountable difficulty. Though Aristotle does not specify the answer to this, a standard criterion for the office of ruler is often age.

Finally, and in full acknowledgment of the fallibility that must attend any particular body of law, given that it is drafted by less than perfectly wise individuals doing the best that they can on the basis of their experience and understanding, Aristotle recognizes the need for law itself to make room and offer a procedure for its correction (see 1287a26-28), thereby allowing even the amendment of law to proceed under the authority of the law.[31]

Conclusion

As he approaches the end of his theoretical reflection on citizen, rule, law, and regime in Book III, Aristotle more directly and emphatically than before underlines his skepticism about both the possibility and the goodness of wisdom in political rule and at the same time highlights his own novel (for his time) solution. First, he declares that the more people who can be involved in each of the offices, the better. Thus he says, "if it is just for the excellent man to rule because he is better, two good persons are better than the one" (1287b14). And again, "it would perhaps be held to be odd if someone should see better with two eyes, judge better with two ears, and act better with two feet and hands than many persons would with many" (1287b26-29). He also returns to re-examine the question of the superiority of wisdom over law, this time saying, "the argument from the example of the arts may be held to be false—namely, that it is a poor thing to heal in accordance with written rules, and one should choose instead to use those who possess the art" (1287a33-35). For, as he goes on to explain, doctors get paid for healing the sick, whereas those involved in "political offices" often have to make decisions where spite or favor or private profit play a role and threaten to override and corrupt even the most learned statesman (1287a36-42). In other words, the political sphere in particular always carries the threat of arousing human beings' passions. The only safeguard against the rule of passion in

---

[31] As for the process for writing a constitution in the first place, Aristotle's own writing in the *Politics* appears to stand as a model and a guide of the kind of discussions and considerations that such an act of legislation requires.

political life is the supremacy of the rule of law which represents "intellect without appetite" (1287a32).

That the law is less than wise and less than precise for every circumstance and situation over which it rules, Aristotle recognizes and acknowledges, as did Plato before him. But in proposing law as constitution—the arrangement of offices—as he does, Aristotle offers a solution that raises the rule of law from a second best solution[32] to the best way for the state to achieve justice and virtue. He does this by turning away from trying to explain what the final end (*telos*) of the political community is, leaving it at the schematic "living well," and turning instead toward identifying the structures and procedures by means of which a political community can work its way toward discovering and defining this end for itself. This allows him at once to account for the lack of wisdom which is the true starting place for every human being, as well as to honor and do justice to the fundamental freedom and capacity for self-rule that is the innate characteristic of human beings.

---

[32] Cf. Plato's *Statesman*, 303b.

2

WHY PUBLIUS?

Mark Shiffman

In crafting a narrative of the beginning of the Roman republic, Plutarch made an unusual choice in giving primary attention to Publius Valerius Publicola rather than the iconic figure of Junius Brutus. Why did Plutarch choose to build his narrative around Publius? Reflection on this question reveals important aspects of Plutarch's thought on the challenges of statesmanship in a republic newly formed by the overthrow of monarchic rule, and of republican statesmanship more generally.

The main sources on the origins of the Roman republic, while they do include Publius in the action, treat Brutus as the far more important figure. Livy generally treats Publius as second fiddle to Brutus and only mentions him a half dozen times after Brutus dies.[1] Dionysius of Halicarnassus mentions him six times in total, whereas he reports speeches by Brutus that span several pages apiece.[2] Plutarch implies that Publius, while Tarquin still rules, is positioning himself for the possibility of a republic, but he still makes Brutus the primary mover and shaper of events. Indeed, when narrating that great archetypal event of republican respect for legality, the presiding of Brutus the consul over the execution of his own sons for treason, Plutarch observes that "the Romans do not deem the work of Romulus in founding the city [*polis*] so great as that of Brutus in bringing about and establishing the republic [*politeia*]."[3] Yet we have a life of

---

[1] Titus Livy, *Ab Urbe Condita*, 2.7.5-12; 2.8.1-3; 2.8.6; 2.11.7-9; 2.16.3-5; 2.16.7-8.

[2] Dionysius of Halicarnassus, *Roman Antiquities*, 4.67; 5.7; 5.13; 5.16; 5.19; 5.48.

[3] Plutarch, *Publicola*, VI.4 (All translations from Plutarch are my own.)

Romulus, but none of Brutus. Perhaps Plutarch implies here that this opinion of the Romans depends upon a trick of perspective, or more properly of chiaroscuro: the glare of Brutus's glory casts into shade the more substantial contributions of Publius. If so, the Life seems designed to correct the illusion.[4]

Plutarch composed the Life of Publius as a parallel to that of Solon. This also raises questions about fitness of choice. Solon is renowned as the great Athenian lawgiver. Publius does make some laws, but in this regard he ranks far behind the earlier kings Numa and Servius, as well as the later composers of the Twelve Tables. There is also an obvious parallel between Solon and Brutus. Solon, to circumvent a law of the war-weary Athenians forbidding anyone to speak of the conquest of Salamis, feigns madness so that he can sing his exhortation with impunity under the inspiration of the Muse.[5] Similarly Brutus obtained his name from the idiocy he had feigned for years so as to remain safe from the jealousies of the tyrants.[6] In Dionysius's account, it is Brutus who puts in place that signature institution of Roman republicanism, the dual office of consul, whereas Plutarch makes the dual office a demand of the demos, who rankled at the very name of king.[7] In either case, Publius had no part in this fundamental original constitutional act, thereby bearing less resemblance to Solon, who does engage in constitutional innovations.[8] Plu-

---

[4] It is worth noting that Cicero, in his reflections on the development of Roman political institutions, speaks only of Publicola when treating of the first years of the republic (*De Re Publica*, II.53-6). Cicero's brief treatment may well have provided the thematic agenda for Plutarch's Life.

[5] *Solon*, VIII.1-2.

[6] *Publicola*, III.4.

[7] *Roman Antiquities*, 73.3-4; *Publicola*, I.4. On the general shift of responsibility for developments in the early republic to Publius from Brutus and others, see Monica Affortunati and Barbara Scardigli, "Aspects of Plutarch's *Life of Publicola*," in *The Statesman in Plutarch's Works, Volume I: Plutarch's Statesman and his Aftermath: Political, Philosophical and Literary Aspects*, edd. Lukas De Blois, Jeroen Bons, Ton Kessels, and Dirk M. Schenkeveld (Leiden: Brill, 2004) 111-2.

[8] *Solon*, XVIII.1-XIX.2. Publius does, however, render the office of consul less dangerous to the public good by instituting the office of quaestor to relieve the consuls of responsibility for public monies (*Publicola*, XII.2).

tarch tells us in the comparison that Publius gave luster to Solon by "setting him up as the most beautiful of paradigms for a man ordering a democratic polity," though within the Life there is no suggestion that Publius knew of Solon or had him in mind as a model.[9]

Furthermore, if we look at the major actions taken over the course of the narrative in the service of founding and securing the new republic, we find that fully one third of them are performed by other actors. Aside from Brutus, who threatens for the first third of the text to eclipse the subject of the Life, we read of several crucial military successes of Publius' brother Marcus Valerius (who seems the better commander of the two), as well as the memorable acts central to the legend of the republican founding performed by the heroic Mucius Scaevola, the intrepid Horatius Cocles, and the daring maiden Cloelia. The only other life in which the primary subject is so little present is the *Lycurgus*. In the latter case, the man disappears into the description, explanation, and praise of his institutions, which is entirely fitting for Lycurgus, the lawgiver par excellence. Indeed, by ending his own life to ensure the permanence of his laws, Lycurgus the mortal man really does disappear into his lawgiving, thereby satisfying what Plato's Socrates's Diotima would describe as an erotic longing for undying honor. Not so Publius, who meets with repeated failures to satisfy his ambitions, and obtains honor largely by the workings of chance and by giving due honor to the actions of others.

Perhaps it is exactly these shortfalls that indicate just why Publius' *Life* is worth writing. The republican ardor of the noble Brutus burns itself out on the battlefield, in the impetuosity of his attack on the son of the expelled tyrant. The legendary deeds of the republican heroes and heroines are singular events bursting forth like fireworks in celebration of the Romans' newfound liberty. The cautious work of stabilizing the new institutions and holding together the newly free people in concord requires a more deliberate temper and less glaring actions. Publius is not the prime mover in the establishing or even institutional shaping of the new republic, but he is the man without

---

[9] *Comparison of Solon and Publicola*, II.1.

whose piecemeal work those institutions might not have survived: "By remaining in the city, and ruling, and engaging in politics, he settled the *politeia* into a stable condition."[10]

Even more important, however, are the reasons why Publius becomes this prudent stabilizer. His numerous missteps, and especially his unfailing ability to recover from them, provide insight into the steep learning curve of the great-souled aristocrat adapting to the eruption of a more democratic spirit in the community. Publius shows himself singularly adept at finding the way to shape his image suitably to the demands of the time without compromising his own dignity. The patrician firebrand of the next generation, Coriolanus, could have learned much from his example.

The key to Publius Valerius Publicola's success is expressed in a line that translators hesitate to render literally. Plutarch tells us that one of his first reforms was to have the lictors (formerly the bodyguard of the king and now attending the consuls) no longer carry their axes while in the city, and to lower their rods before the *demos* when entering the popular assembly with the consul. Plutarch's gloss on this innovation is that Publius was "making a great *show* of democracy."[11] While "*proschema*" can in certain contexts be translated as "dignity," it strains the syntax of this passage to take it otherwise than in its overwhelmingly dominant meaning of "pretense" or "screen." After noting that the consuls have preserved the same practice to his own day (that is to say, over six hundred years later), Plutarch remarks quite explicitly: "The multitude did not see that he was not, as they thought, abasing himself, but rather purging and preventing their envy by this moderation, adding to the greatness of his power exactly to the extent that he seemed to relinquish his authority."[12] His reform

---

[10] Ibid, III.3.

[11] *Publicola*, X.5. The Dryden translation renders the clause: "to show, in the strongest way, the republican foundation of the government." *Plutarch's Lives*, translated by John Dryden (Modern Library, 2001) 135. The Loeb gives: "emphasizing the majesty of the democracy." Plutarch, *Lives*, translated by Bernadotte Perrin (Cambridge: Harvard University Press, 1914) 529.

[12] Ibid., X.6.

of the symbolism of the lictors is the first institutional signal that Publius has understood the essential predicament of the citizen-statesman in a republic.

What is this predicament? To be truly worthy to rule, a man must possess superior virtue. In a republic, he must convince his fellow citizens, on whom his advancement depends, that he possesses such virtue. But the defining feature of a republic, that the citizens rule and are ruled in turn, implies a certain equality in principle among the citizens. The superior man thus has to show himself worthy of rule while appearing neither too eager to rule (lest he arouse suspicion of tyrannical ambitions) nor too conscious of his superiority (lest he arouse the envy of the inferior, who resent that superiority[13]). This is exactly the predicament Publius is caught in after the expulsion of the Tarquins and the beginning of the republic; it is by learning to steer his way through this predicament that he becomes a paradigmatic figure for the republican citizen-statesman. Let us examine how Plutarch charts this trajectory.

The first thing we learn about Publius Valerius is that he was honored by the demos with the title Publicola, "lover of the people." We next learn of his distinguished ancestry, traceable to the time of Romulus: his ancestor Valerius was, more than anyone else, responsible for turning the original Romans and the Sabines, at first enemies, into a single demos—a feat he accomplished by working at the highest level, reconciling the two kings. Plutarch sounds a principal theme of the Life by using the word "demos" twice in the first sentence; it appears five times in the first two paragraphs, along with one instance of "demokratia." The relationship of Publius to the demos of Rome is fundamental to the story.

But what is meant by the demos? Does the word refer to the non-aristocratic many, as typical in Greek philosophical usage? Or does it refer to the whole body of Romans, as it seems to in the se-

---

[13] For a general treatment of envy in the *Lives*, see Alan Wardman, *Plutarch's Lives* (Berkeley and Los Angeles: University of California Press, 1974) 69-78.

cond instance? Presumably Plutarch, even if he has not yet written the Life of Romulus, is aware of what he tells us there, that even before the absorption of the Sabines, Romulus had established the patricians as a distinct order within the city;[14] yet Plutarch here uses "demos" as if it applies to all the conglomerated Romans and Sabines, perhaps excluding only the kings. This lack of clarity would seem to point to the challenge that will face Publius: to foster the sense among patricians and plebeians that they are a single people. But is a man of such distinguished ancestry the right man for such a task?

The way Publius bears himself under the monarchy initially seems to suggest that he may indeed promise to be that man:

> Related by lineage to such a man, Valerius, so they say, while Rome was still ruled by kings, was conspicuous both for his speech and for his wealth; and since he employed the former rightly and with frankness always on behalf of just things, and from the latter he provided the needy liberally and philanthropically, it was clear from the start that if a democracy were to come about, he was going to be one of the first men.[15]

The hypothetical possibility of a future democracy coming into being (*ei genoito demokratia*) is both suggestive and underdetermined. Are we to think Publius hoped for a democracy or envisioned the possibility? Or is this observation a retrospective assessment of how his actions and stature under the monarchy ought to have positioned him for leadership in the new regime?

If Publius did envision a new regime, we have no sign of it. Brutus is the one who seizes the opportunity and recruits Publius into the leadership of the overthrow. Our major sources agree on this: Publius formed part of the revolutionary nucleus because he was trusted by fellow patricians in the circle around Lucretia's husband Collatinus, while it was the vehement resolution of Brutus that set the coup in motion. More importantly, if the status of Publius should have led

---

[14] *Romulus*, XIII.2.
[15] *Publicola*, I.2.

naturally to prominence in the new order, this expectation is disappointed:

> As long as it looked like the demos was going to select one man as general in place of the king, Valerius kept calm, considering it more fitting for Brutus to rule, having been the leader of the liberation. But when (the name of monarchy being offensive) the demos considered it less painful to submit to a partitioned rule, and proposed and resolved upon two offices, he, hoping to be chosen along with Brutus as co-consul, failed entirely to obtain it.[16]

This failure, despite the fact that Brutus, the popular hero, supported him over Collatinus, suggests both that Publius was at least disposed to hope for prominence all along, and that the favor he had earned under the monarchy (which seemed to promise it) no longer stands him in good stead, despite his prominent role in expelling the tyrant. Brutus may trust him more than anyone, but the Romans apparently do not.

What has happened? Quite simply, the regime has changed. Under the monarchy, Publius maintained an independent status and power based on his wealth and patrician standing, and from that high personal station could provide the less powerful and wealthy with a bulwark against oppression. With the disappearance of the monarchic power and the inauguration of a republic, this same independent power and status becomes a potential threat to the new order. The other powerful men don't consider him as reliable an opponent of a restoration as the injured Collatinus, and the people seem to share in the uncertainty about him sufficiently to oppose the wishes of Brutus. The very superiority of stature that made him popular under the monarchy makes him suspect in the republic.

No longer rewarded with the confidence of his fellow Romans, Publius ceases engaging in the actions by which he formerly earned it: he "kept away from the Senate, renounced his pleadings on behalf of others, and entirely left off his public activities, occasioning both remark and concern to the multitude, who feared that, attaching him-

---

[16] Ibid., I.4.

self to the royals, he might overturn their affairs and the precariously situated polis."[17] Has he withdrawn in a fit of disgust, aggravated that all his careful positioning has come to naught? Or has he decided to put the Romans in mind of the value of his good will? Either way, his next action reassures his fellow citizens: when Brutus proposes that the patricians all take an oath of loyalty in the Senate, Publius is the *first* to take the oath to battle with all his might for their freedom.[18] With this dramatic gesture, he takes the first step toward becoming a masterful craftsman and curator of his republican image, in a way that simultaneously reminds the Romans of his importance and demonstrates his responsiveness to their anxieties and wishes. Further, his advice to the Senators not to allow the newly arrived envoys of the Tarquins to speak before the multitude of poorer citizens, who "felt war to be a heavier burden than tyranny," shows that his long association with the needy bears fruit in a sensibility of their passions that allows him to read and effectively manage them.

In his successful reconciliation of himself to both the people and the patricians, Publius manages to exemplify something of the essence of political representation, which is part of the genius of Roman political life. Publius goes from being a focus of anxiety over division within the city to a representative of its unity in opposition to tyranny; and he brings about this change because he is both responsive to the popular feeling and at the same time able to exercise his own judgment to prevent popular feeling from swaying deliberations over good policy. He thus becomes an exemplar of what a republic needs: public figures who represent the unified will of the community but act on superior judgment.

A chance occurrence provides a further occasion for his past habits to pay off. When the slave Vindicius overhears the sons of both Brutus and Collatinus plotting a restoration, he is too frightened to reveal it to the consuls, since they are fathers to the conspirators. Not knowing where to go, but knowing that he has to tell someone, Vin-

---

[17] Ibid., II.1.
[18] Ibid., II.2.

dicius "somehow turned toward Valerius, drawn by the philanthropic acts for the commoners of this man who was easy for all the needy to approach."[19] The choice is not immediately obvious, but highly effective, the result proving how easy it remains for Publius to act on his own independent resources, and how careful he is to have the means to justify his actions. The first thing he does is lock Vindicius up in a room in his house, presumably to be sure not to lose the witness to his grounds for unilateral action. Then he sets out for the house of the conspirators with "the multitude [of clients] and friends who were always about him, and a retinue of attendants."[20] Still a man of wealth and consequence, he has enough hangers-on to force an entry into the private home of one of Rome's most important families, and does so on his own initiative.

A very public scene follows as the Valerii drag the conspirators to the Forum. When Brutus absents himself after the execution of his own sons, Collatinus, the remaining consul, begins to take a soft line on the other miscreants and acquiesces in the demand for the return of their slave. Publius, neither willing to lose face by handing over Vindicius, now "mingled in among the crowd about him," nor "to permit the demos to let off the young men and depart," calls back Brutus, who denounces Collatinus.[21] Publius has seized the moment of his exemplary public service and proof of loyalty and seen it through to its end before the eyes of the demos. Upon the dismissal of Collatinus, Publius "reaps the worthy recompense of his zeal" when in the new election he is proclaimed consul "*lampros*"—here primarily meaning "decisively," but bearing overtones of "splendidly," "radiantly" and "illustriously." Having finally demonstrated his republican credentials, Publius once again enjoys his exalted stature in the public heart and eye.

Soon, however, he is alone in the public eye, and before long this begins to estrange him from the public heart. In the first battle of the

---

[19] Ibid., IV.4
[20] Ibid., V.1.
[21] Ibid., VII.2.

new republic against the Tarquins and their Etruscan allies, Brutus
meets his death. The two armies, after being forced apart by a storm,
hear a mysterious booming voice declaring that the Etruscans had lost
one man more than the Romans—which caused cheers from the Romans and flight in the Etruscans.[22] For this "victory" Publius cele-
brates the first consular triumph in "august and magnificent" style
driving a four-horse chariot. Plutarch notes that some claim that this
novel pomp was vexing and excited envy, but dismisses the claim on
the grounds that consuls continued the practice for countless years.
Publius also delivers a gracious encomium to Brutus that delights the
Romans and sets another long-honored precedent.[23]

The dual precedent established here, of magnificent consular
triumphs and of honoring the republic's deceased "good and great
men," merits close scrutiny. If Publius' magnificence in this instance
does not excite criticism (whereas his magnificence in office soon
will), there seem to be two likely reasons. First, the Romans, ecstatic
at their deliverance, seem to be celebrating themselves rather than
their marginally responsible consul in this public festival. Second,
Publius' companion innovation, honoring the beloved hero Brutus in
a marvelous public encomium, seems calculated to deflect from Publius the danger of seeming to concentrate too much glory on himself.
In both cases, he manages simultaneously to appear as both a man of
superior stature and merit, and also merely the embodiment of Roman republican liberty and virtue.

At the same time, his primary achievement in the battle seems to
have been not dying. After all, had he imitated the ardent zeal of Brutus, the Romans might not have lost one man fewer than the Etruscans. This conjunction of episodes, then, illustrates the essence of
Publius' statesmanship: by prudently surviving to continuously represent Roman republicanism, he establishes practices in the conduct of
consular office that shape the way republican Rome represents itself
to itself through its highest public officers. In the triumph, later con-

[22] Ibid., IX.4.
[23] Ibid., IX.5-7.

40

suls vie with earlier to represent the republic's achievements more magnificently (spurring them to more magnificent achievements for the republic); in the encomia, prominent public men show their eloquence and discretion by honoring other prominent public men in a tradition of virtuous conduct. Love of honor comes to be firmly embedded in and supportive of the republican practice of vying for virtue within the framework of ruling and being ruled in turn.

The balance of personal greatness and republican representativeness achieved in this dual precedent is, however, very quickly eclipsed in the public eye and heart by the very un-republican image Publius presents as he continues in office without replacing Brutus with another co-consul. The stature he assumes for himself takes a very visible form which Plutarch, attributing words to the demos, contrasts explicitly with Publius' encomium:

> "Why should he commemorate Brutus in speech while imitating Tarquin in deed, descending alone, accompanied by all the rods and axes, from a house equal in grandeur to the king's that he demolished?" For indeed, Valerius dwelt in a very grand [*tragikoteron*] house on the so-called Velia, looming over the Forum and overlooking from on high all that happened there, steep and difficult to approach from its environs, so that the spectacle of his descent was in elevated style, and the majesty of his accompanying procession kingly.[24]

Publius is warned by frank-speaking friends that he "seemed to the many to be transgressing [*hamartanein*]." The fact that he requires this warning suggests that the concern of the people is not without merit, that his grandeur is beginning to render him oblivious of their moods. Publius resolves on the grandest gesture of his career: he has workmen come in the middle of the night and razes the house to its foundations.

> Consequently the Romans, seeing it in the morning and gathering together, loved [*agapan*] and admired [*thaumazein*] the greatness of the man's thoughts, but were grieved for the house and mourned

---

[24] Ibid., X.2.

the greatness and beauty of it, as though it were human, now that it had been unjustly destroyed through envy, and also for their ruler, who like a homeless man was now dwelling in the houses of others.[25]

This simple gesture is complex in its resonance. The envy felt by the people presupposes a jealous love for the house, a love covered over by anger. The loss of this beloved beauty renders the people sympathetic to its possessor's love and his loss; this is a point on which they can identify with the otherwise distant aristocrat. The loss, again, simultaneously demonstrates his responsiveness to their anxieties and his true superiority in sacrificing this ornament of Rome to earn their trust. The sacrifice is, as it were, an act of high munificence, an aristocratic citizen giving the centerpiece of his wealth and stability for the good of the republic. That act of munificence, calculated to purge and prevent demotic envy, is what is now most visible as they conduct their affairs every day in the Forum.

The subtle precision of Plutarch's language underscores a deeper register of this magnificent act. The demos, faulting Publius for living in as splendid a house as Tarquin's, cast him as the agent of the latter's destruction, as if he had enviously eliminated the rival to his own grand edifice: *he* tore down [*katheile*] Tarquin's house. In Plutarch's earlier narration of that destruction, however, there is considerable ambiguity regarding who is responsible for the destruction of the royal residence: the consuls "gave the goods of the kings to the Romans to plunder, and they razed [*kateskapsan*] the house."[26] The subject of this plural verb could be either the consuls or the Romans, or both, but certainly not Publius alone (though he is one of the consuls). When, however, he destroys his own house, he is the singular subject of the same verb: "quickly gathering a multitude of workmen, while it was night he threw down the house and razed [*kateskapsen*] the whole thing to its foundation."[27]

---

[25] Ibid, X.4.
[26] Ibid., VIII.1.
[27] Ibid., X.3.

In the destruction of the Tarquin palace, the consuls and the people are in a sense interchangeable: if the consuls order or permit its destruction, they do so as the representatives of popular anger and envy, its official voice and ratification. When Publius becomes the target of the demos' envy, they project their own envy of Tarquin onto him, describing him as the single agent of an emphatically and absurdly physical act of pulling down the building. The description of Publius' response suggests that he takes valuable lessons from both episodes: he takes singular responsibility for carrying out on his own house what he had permitted the demos to do to Tarquin's. He thus simultaneously acts as executor of popular envy and suffers as its victim, fusing together admiration for his grandeur, gratitude for his sacrifice, compassion for his vulnerability, and identification with his representative agency. It would be difficult to imagine an act that more perfectly exemplifies successfully managing the image problem of the republican citizen-statesman of superior merit and stature—an act demonstrating how a statesman can simultaneously act as representative of the people and secure his superior stature on the ground of superior merit.[28]

It is worth taking note of the continuing but changed role that buildings play in the subsequent narrative. The temple of Capitoline Jupiter, which became the preeminent temple of the city, was built by Tarquin, who was deposed before it could be dedicated. Publius, Plutarch tells us, harbored an ambition [*philotimia*] to dedicate it in his consulship.[29] This time he is crossed by the envy of his peers (literally, "the many of the powerful"), who consider his honors for his lawgiving and generalship quite a sufficient share, and manage affairs so that his co-consul obtains the privilege of dedicating the temple. This new focus of his love of honor, to have his name permanently attached to a

---

[28] This exemplary act seems to have required some imagination on Plutarch's part: in both Livy (2.7.5-12) and Dionysius (5.19) the house is under construction and the grumblings occasion a change of location. Plutarch has it that, after he takes up rotating abode with various friends, the compassionate demos provides him a new location and a more modest house (X.4).

[29] *Publicola*, XIV.1.

prominent public building, evinces a kind of republican sublimation: rather than enjoying immediate personal visibility among his contemporaries such as his grand house afforded him, Publius now seeks immortal remembrance among the Romans in connection with a civic monument—but cannot attain it precisely because he cannot escape the contest of emulation among the patriciate, the healthy agonism that produces virtuous statesmen. At least, it produces virtuous statesmen as long as the health of the republic lasts—which Plutarch calls to mind in a digression about the subsequent demolitions and rebuildings of this temple. There he tells us that the one here dedicated lasted until the civil wars, the second was built by the sanguinary dictator Sulla, the third by the not-so-bad emperor Vespasian, and the fourth by the tastelessly extravagant emperor Domitian, who suffered from a "disease of building."[30]

The mention of this disease highlights the lapse of prudence involved in Publius' next building project, described in the subsequent paragraph. When the Etruscan king Porsenna is marching on Rome to restore Tarquin, Publius, in order to show that he surpasses Porsenna in grandeur of thought, builds and garrisons the city of Sigliura! The fall of this seemingly ill-conceived first line of defense nearly brings the Etruscans into the gate of Rome.[31] Publius cannot be Romulus, the founder of the city who is worshipped as a god. In seeking republican analogues, having both a temple and a city associated forever with his name, he momentarily loses a firm grip on the immediate practical exigencies.

These disappointments in the pursuit of lasting fame embodied in buildings give place, in the remainder of the narrative, to the memorable actions of others in the defense of the republic. The penumbra of these events, however, is the final attainment of republican statesmanship by Publius: he comes to excel at honoring, supporting and recognizing the excellence of others. When the Etruscans press hard toward the city that Publius' town-building has put in danger, Hora-

---

[30] Ibid., XV.
[31] Ibid., XVI.1-4.

tius Cocles heroically fends them off while the Romans dismantle the bridge behind him. When Publius convinces the Romans to honor him publicly, it shows his willingness to share glory, and probably eclipses their consul's lack of judgment in their memories as well. Porsenna's admiration of his would-be assassin Mucius Scaevola may have suggested to Publius the trustworthiness of the Etruscan king as an arbitrator with Tarquin—a proposal which leads to an estrangement between the upright Etruscan and the exile king who disdains his arbitration. Publius supports and counsels his brother Marcus in his consulship, in which the latter achieves a stunning military victory, a triumph and lasting public honors.

When in his final consulship the Sabines and Latins form a confederacy that threatens Rome, Publius recognizes a potential ally in the archetypal aristocrat Appius Claudius, whose situation recalls that of Publius at the beginning of the republic: "a man powerful because of his wealth, illustrious for his bodily vigor, and preeminent for his reputation for virtue and the brilliance of his speech, he was unable to escape the fate of great men, but was envied—those who envied him charging (because he was trying to prevent the war) that he meant to increase the Roman power with a view to tyrannizing and enslaving his own country."[32] As Claudius primes his considerable retinue to resist his countrymen, Publius invites him, rather than warring with his own, to take refuge in Rome, promising to receive him with honors—"public and private"—worthy of his virtue, and of the splendor of Rome. The accession of this noble house, admitted immediately to the Senate, brings to Rome one of its most illustrious patrician families (a sometimes troublesome mainstay of the aristocratic republic for generations), and at the same time puts an end to the immediate threat from Rome's neighbors.

In rescuing Appius Claudius from the menace of envy, Publius demonstrates that he has mastered the art of deflecting envy from himself. By honoring the actions of republican heroes, supporting the glory of his deserving brother, and bringing to Rome an illustrious

---

[32] Ibid., XXI.2.

double of his former self, Publius places himself conspicuously in the shadow of their splendor. There he appears as the constant guiding presence that sustains Rome's ability to be the glorious republic in which its citizens can take pride. Having first mastered the art of representing Rome's republicanism to itself in his own superior person, he also masters the discipline of gaining honor through granting honors to the numerous virtuous characters the republic needs to populate it and sustain its faith in itself.

As the destruction of his house consummately exemplifies his art of representative preeminence, so the final honors granted him upon his death (which echo that event) exemplify his less visible (or conspicuously invisible) sustaining presence:

> The demos, just as though they had done none of the things he deserved while he was living, but still owed him every favor, voted to entomb his body at public expense, and that each should contribute a quarter-obol as an honor.... And likewise by vote of the citizens, he was buried within the confines of the city, beside the so-called Velian, with the intention that all his gens would have a share in burial there. Today, however, no one of his latter-day gens is buried there; but once the corpse is carried and set down there and someone, taking a torch, holds it under it for a moment, it is then removed—by this act attesting to the privilege, and to the relinquishing of this honor.[33]

At the foot of the very same outcropping of the Palatine hill atop which his house had stood, the Romans provide him at public expense a home for all time, where he remains a constant and silent presence right next to the Forum—a republican memorialization of a man who taught the republic how to honor its heroes. Publius thus attains from the republic the monument he longed for in a public edifice, one by which he remains forever one who represents the republic in his life and death. Meanwhile the corpses of his latter-day descendants re-enact his relinquishing of his original honorable dwelling place.

---

[33] Ibid., XXIII. 2–3.

The destruction of the house, leaving a visible absence in the republican landscape, and the presence of the tomb, making visible the absence of the man, aptly symbolize the trick of perspective of Publicola's statesmanship, his constant presence in the penumbra of the most visible events and symbols. Thus the "appearance of democracy" resulting from the removal of the lictors' axes and the lowering of their rods in the presence of the assembled people is not simply a ruse for maintaining power. These gestures reassure the demos that the republic recognizes their will and dignity, even if not their equal merit. In a similar if potentially more substantive gesture, Publius made any citizen eligible for the consulship; nonetheless, patricians were almost always elected. Even while in principle his reforms granted them representation in the highest office, they ceded minimal scope in the direction of policy and legislation. For nearly four hundred years, Rome maintained its character as an aristocratic republic, able to make concessions to the people while never ceasing to be effectively governed by noble families with distinguished traditions of virtue, public service and farsightedness.[34] Men like Publius could continue to be Rome's first citizens, while the multitude could share and participate in the dignity of citizenship, a dignity whose tone continued to be set to a high standard by the patrician officers who represented the republic to itself.

The trick of perspective in this period is not, however, all the doing of Publius. While prudent concessions to the plebeians, partly symbolic and partly substantive, help to maintain a sense of unity in the Roman people, this esprit de corps is supported by the real common cause of resisting Tarquin's effort to restore the monarchy. In the next generation, as dramatized in the Life of Coriolanus, the conflict of the orders comes to the forefront of Roman politics, and comes to be embodied institutionally in the newly created office of the Tribunes of the Plebs. Coriolanus, a child when the republic is

---

[34] Cf. Cicero, *De Re Publica*, II.55: "This, in my judgment, was no mediocre man who, by giving a measured liberty to the people, more easily maintained the authority of the first men." (Loeb, 166, my translation.)

founded, comes of age in the battle that ends the threat of Tarquin, and finds cause, after the creation of the Tribunes, to lament the lost unity of the city and to predict its increasing polarization as the Tribunes pursue their ambitions of encroachment on the Senatorial regime.[35] Thus in Plutarch the first decades of the republic play out *in nuce* the drama of the glory days of unity against the Carthaginian threat and the unbalancing of the republic in the Tribuneships of the Gracchi.

In the comparison, Plutarch highlights Solon's great debt relief as the keystone of his stabilization of the citizens' liberties.[36] He does not explicitly remark that Publicola fails to follow his purported model in this regard. It is, however, exactly the problem of debt that leads to the crisis in which the Tribunes are created as a concession to the revolted Plebs.[37] After the creation of the Tribunes, whose ambitions can only be satisfied by agitations against the Senatorial regime, it is no longer possible for anyone to represent the unity of the city as deftly and effectively as Publius was able to do, except in the extraordinary office of the Dictator in times of extreme crisis. While Publius cannot strictly be faulted for failing to foresee the kind of crisis that Solon had to respond to (hence Plutarch's refusal to explicitly reproach him), his failure to forestall the problem of debt opened the fissure between the orders that he had managed to keep closed, or at least to paper over. As a result, his political legacy amplifies his achievement in life: as a statesman able to represent the unity of the republic in his person, he remains an inescapably superior paradigm for Roman consuls of the following ages.

---

[35] *Caius Martius Coriolanus*, III.1, XVI.4.
[36] *Comparison of Solon and Publicola*, III.1.
[37] *Caius Martius Coriolanus*, V.1-3, VII.1.

PART II

ON MODERN REPUBLICANISM

3

MONTAIGNE AND MODERN REPUBLICANISM

Benjamin Storey

A study of Michel de Montaigne's *Essays* seems a distinctly unpromising avenue to a better understanding of modern republicanism. Montaigne's book, written in the last decades of the sixteenth century, seems to be a disordered collection of chapters about most everything: thumbs, cannibals, sleep, smells. Everything, that is, except politics: in the *Essays,* there is no chapter "Of Hereditary Principalities," as there is in Machiavelli's *Prince,* or "Of the Commonwealth," as in Hobbes's *Leviathan,* or "Of the Ends of Political Society and Government," as in Locke's *Second Treatise.* There is no "Of Republics." The *Essays* has been rightly called a cornucopian text, a text overflowing with gratuitous insight into every imaginable aspect of life—except the political matters of ruling and being ruled.[1] Insofar as the modern political philosophy which helps create modern republicanism consists in a new, systematic account of natural right or the proper organization of political institutions, Montaigne does not seem to contribute anything at all.

There is, however, at least circumstantial evidence for the view that Montaigne is not irrelevant to modern republicanism. The great modern political philosophers—Hobbes, Locke, Montesquieu, Rousseau, Tocqueville, and Nietzsche—all read Montaigne and learned from him. In fact, the *Essays* are thought to have been the most popular book in Europe during the 17th century, and continued to fascinate readers like Voltaire and Diderot in the 18th, the *siècle des lu-*

---

[1] Terence Cave, *The Cornucopian Text: Problems of Writing in the French Renaissance* (Oxford: Oxford University Press, 1979).

mières, the century that issued in the modern republican revolutions.[2] Montaigne has long been of great interest to modern republicans, in spite of the apparently apolitical character of the *Essays*. Why has this apparently apolitical writer drawn so much attention from those who put politics at the center of their thought? Because Montaigne articulates a moral vision, a vision of the good life, that is at the heart of modern republicanism precisely because it is apolitical. He articulates an understanding of the relation between the private and the public that puts the private first. As they elaborated their accounts of natural right and effective republican political institutions, the modern political philosophers would follow Montaigne in this fundamental reversal of the order of priorities between the private and the public. Sound understanding of modern republicanism therefore depends on our understanding of the nature and significance of this reversal.

Montaigne's new understanding of the relation between the private and the public is rooted in his new understanding of the relation between nature and custom, and indeed on his new understanding of nature as such. Montaigne inaugurates a view of nature that will have great influence in modern life: he is the first to see nature as a non-teleological moral standard, as an ethical guide but not a form of perfection. This understanding of nature is implicitly antinomian and anti-political. Montaignean nature is a moral standard of private life, which he understands as a refuge for the practice of new and decidedly modern virtues: nonchalance, frankness, authenticity, and humanity. He sees politics, by contrast, as an arena of irrational, even inhuman, ambition, and he consigns law to the status of irrational, if necessary, custom.

Montaigne is, in short, a specifically modern counterpoint to another great modern, Machiavelli; modern republicanism oscillates between the two poles of this opposition.[3] Insofar as we are modern

---

[2] Marc Fumaroli, *La querelle des anciens et des modernes* (Paris: Gallimard, 2001) 9.

[3] On this point, see Kevin S. Honeycutt, "Eschatological Dissatisfaction: Montaigne's Response to Machiavelli on Fortune and Death" in *No Greater Monster or Miracle than Myself: The Political Philosophy of Michel de Montaigne*, ed.

republicans, we cannot understand ourselves without understanding the tension between Machiavellian political amoralism and antinaturalism and Montaigne's new standard of non-teleological yet moral naturalism, the moral naturalism of private life.

Montaigne, the Classical and Christian Traditions, and Machiavelli

To understand the significance of Montaigne's nonteleological moral naturalism for modern republicanism, we have to understand him in relation to the classical and Christian tradition, on the one hand, and Machiavelli on the other. His contribution is best understood in its opposition to these rival views of the relation between nature, law, morality, and politics.

For Aristotle, nature, law, morality, and politics are tied together in a knot whose threads pull in conflicting directions but can never be fully untied. Man is by nature a political animal, Aristotle tells us, but the founder of the first city is a great benefactor of mankind: that is, cities are both natural and a work of artifice. We can understand this paradoxical pair of assertions in the light of another paradox: Aristotle asserts that man apart from politics is either a beast or a god. That is, without politics, we would either be subhuman or superhuman. [4]

Man has, for Aristotle, a natural perfection, a *telos*. He cannot reach this *telos* without education, without the soul-shaping influence of law, law that habituates us to virtue. Apart from the virtue-inculcating habituation of law, we would be beastly and even worse than beastly. We cannot achieve the flourishing that is possible for us by nature without substantial help from art; we are like lilies that put forth magnificent flowers but require stakes to grow up straight. And

---

Charlotte C. S. Thomas (Macon: Mercer University Press, 2014) and contrast David Lewis Schaefer, who describes Montaigne as Machiavelli's "first philosophic follower." "Montaigne, Tocqueville, and the Politics of Skepticism," *Perspectives on Political Science* (Fall 2002, Volume 31, no. 4) 205; see also Schaefer, *The Political Philosophy of Montaigne* (Ithaca: Cornell University Press, 1990).

[4] Aristotle, *Politics*, 1253a1-40.

yet custom is always custom, not nature; custom distorts nature even as it helps it do its work. The most perfect human being is the most godlike, and as such transcends politics; custom holds us back from that transcendence.

With some important variations, Thomas Aquinas adopts the Aristotelian view: he sees law and politics as playing a decisive role in helping man achieve his natural *telos* or perfection.[5] Both Aristotle and Aquinas, in somewhat different ways, measure human political orders and laws against the yardstick of nature, as is most clearly articulated in Aquinas's argument that a human law that does not accord with the natural law is no law at all.[6] Teleological nature is, for both, a standard for politics, and we need politics and law to achieve our natural perfection.

Departing from the classical and Christian tradition, Machiavelli rejects nature as a moral and political standard. Nature has no ethical authority, he thinks—perhaps ultimately because he does not think nature was created by an intelligent and beneficent God. He therefore argues that a prince should *change his nature* if that is what political necessity dictates as expedient. Nature is as blind and dumb as fortune, and it wants to kill us. We should resist it as long as possible and conquer it if we can.[7] As for human life, it is political all the way down. Machiavelli divides the human world into two kinds of men: those who desire to acquire power, wealth, and glory and do so successfully, and those who desire to acquire those things but fail. We are all hammers or anvils, masters or slaves, conquerors or conquered. Most deeply, politics itself is merely war by other means.[8] Machiavelli's teaching can be summed in his Promethean call to conquer fortune if we can. We cannot rely on anyone—nature, God, or other

---

[5] Thomas Aquinas, *Summa Theologiae*, IaIIae 95:1.

[6] Ibid., IaIIae 95:2.

[7] Machiavelli, *Prince*, tr. Harvey C. Mansfield (Chicago: University of Chicago Press, 1998) 98-100.

[8] Ibid., p. 14-15, 48, 69.

human beings—to love us or care for us. We can only rely on our-selves.[9] Politics is where the action is; nature is no guide for man.

Montaigne rejects the classical and Christian tradition and Machiavelli at once. Like Machiavelli, he argues that "imaginary, arti-ficial descriptions of a government prove ridiculous and unfit to put into practice" (III.9.887).[10] But Montaigne "mortally hates" Machia-vellianism, and marks his disagreements with Machiavelli himself on several occasions (see II.17.596-597 and III.1, entire). The trajectory of the *Essays* is a headlong flight from the Machiavellian political world of ambition, artifice, dissimulation, war, and cruelty into a pri-vate life of humane, nonchalant authenticity and frankness, which takes its moral guidance from what Montaigne calls "the good coun-sels of our mother Nature" (I.20.81).

Montaignean Nature as a Nonteleological Moral Standard

What does it mean to take nature as a nonteleological moral stand-ard? In one of the most memorable images of the *Essays*, Montaigne writes:

> Men have done with Nature as perfumers do with oil: they have so-phisticated her with so many arguments and farfetched reasonings that she has become variable and particular for each man, and has lost her own constant and universal countenance; and we must seek in the animals evidence of her that is not subject to favor, corrup-tion, or diversity of opinion. (III.9.978)

The teleological nature of the ancients is, for Montaigne, an adulterated, artificial nature—a nature reeking of cheap cologne. When men want to perfect themselves, when they strive to be godlike or angelic, Montaigne writes that "instead of changing themselves into angels, they change themselves into beasts; instead of raising themselves, they lower themselves" (III.13.1044). The human search

---

[9] Ibid., p. 101, 97.

[10] Citations of the *Essays* refer to *The Complete Works of Michel de Mon-taigne*, tr. Donald M. Frame (New York: Knopf, 2003) and give book, chapter, and page numbers.

for perfection is not natural but the reverse; it is an inhuman desire to transcend ourselves that masks and does violence to our nature.

For Montaigne, the human problem, the "commonest of human errors," as he puts it, is not knowing how to be "at home" (I.3.9). The classical and Christian tradition worried that man would fall into, or even below, beastliness—like the Cyclops devouring sheep and men in his cave—without the civilizing influence of law and custom to guide us toward our natural perfection. Montaigne's concern is precisely the reverse: the dangerous and typical human tendency is not falling too low but flying too high. He is worried less about the Cyclops than about Icarus.

From Montaigne's perspective, Machiavelli and his classical and Christian predecessors have important things in common. We can see this in one of his descriptions of the autobiographical mode of writing he practices in the *Essays*: whereas "authors communicate with the people by some special extrinsic mark," he tells us, "I am the first to do so by my entire being, as Michel de Montaigne, not as a grammarian or a poet or a jurist" (III.2.741). He speaks as a human being simply, not as any one type of human being, any particular model of human perfection.

Montaigne here takes aim at some easy targets—grammarians, poets, and jurists. But his argument implies a more daring assault on more revered human standards. Montaigne makes plain, in the *Essays*, that he aspires to neither the holiness of the saint nor the heroism of the citizen; he regards maintaining only a loose attachment to his Catholicism and his country as a virtue (III.2.748; III.13.1000). He also remarks that he is "no philosopher" (III.9.881; II.6.332). All of the ways of life celebrated by the classical and Christian tradition aim at forms of perfection Montaigne sees as distortions of our humanity. He presents himself merely as Michel de Montaigne, not as philosopher, citizen, or saint.

He also has no ambition to be a prince. For Montaigne, Machiavellian political ambition—like the saintly, civic, and philosophic forms of heroism celebrated by the classical and Christian tradition—is a perverse attempt to rise above our humanity. Montaigne encapsulates his critique of political ambition in his many discussions of Alexander the Great, who figures, from the beginning to the end of the *Essays*, as a negative example, a man who does not know how to be content with the measure of a man (I.1.5-6; III.2.745; III.13.1044). Machiavellian political ambition, Socratic philosophic ambition, the religious ambition of a St. Augustine, the civic ambition of Cato—to Montaigne, they are all examples of the human tendency to try to rise above ourselves, which ultimately makes men monstrous. Montaigne's critique of these models of dehumanizing perfection can be summed up in the dark irony with which he tells the story of Cato committing suicide by disemboweling himself rather than submitting to Caesar. Cato's virtue is a kind of masochistic delight in his own pain (II.11.374).[11]

Montaigne attacks the determined seriousness, the single-mindedness, of all human pursuits of perfection as unnatural. As he writes in the chapter *Of Vanity*, which self-consciously reverses the teaching of Ecclesiastes:

> A single cord never keeps me in place. 'There is vanity,' you say, 'in this amusement.' But where is there not? And these fine precepts are vanity, and all wisdom is vanity. *The Lord knoweth the thoughts of the wise, that they are vain.* These exquisite subtleties are only fit for preaching; they are arguments that would send us all saddled into the other world. Life is a material and corporeal movement, and action which by its very essence is imperfect and irregular; I apply myself to serving it in its own way. (III.9.919)

Montaigne's nonteleological moral naturalism emphasizes movement and variety over steadiness of purpose. It emphasizes corporeality over spirituality. And, as indicated above, Montaigne would have us look to the animals for guidance as to how to live, rather than to the gods.

---

[11] See Paul Rahe, *Republics Ancient and Modern* (Chapel Hill: University of North Carolina Press, 1994) Volume II, 40.

Montaigne thus initiates a second tradition of modern political philosophy that stands in contrapuntal tension with the hyperpolitical Prometheanism of Machiavelli and his followers. In this, he is a forerunner of Rousseau, who, in his *Second Discourse*, turns to nature in reaction to the civilizing but corrupting forces of the Enlightenment, and argues that the more natural we are, the closer to the animals we are, the better we are. These two strains—Machiavellian Prometheanism on the one hand, Montaignean non-teleological moral naturalism on the other—are the poles of what is perhaps the most basic dynamic of disagreement that propels both modern political philosophy and modern political life.

The Virtues of Montaignean Naturalism

One might wonder what nature as a non-teleological moral standard even means. After all, isn't every quest to live morally a striving toward some sort of perfection? How can artless anti-perfectionism be a moral standard? We can best understand the moral possibility of naturalism without perfectionism by considering, in succession, four novel virtues that Montaigne exemplifies in his own person: nonchalance, authenticity, frankness, and humanity.[12]

Montaigne articulates his case for what he calls *nonchaloir*, nonchalance, most strikingly with respect to death. As he writes in *That to Philosophize is to Learn to Die*: "I want death to find me planting my cabbages, but careless of her [*nonchalant d'elle*], and still more of my unfinished garden" (I.20.74). This studied carelessness about death extends to all other aspects of life:

> In household management, in study, in hunting, and in all other pursuits, we should take part up to the utmost limits of pleasure, but beware of engaging ourselves further, where it begins to be mingled with pain. We must reserve only so much business and occupation as we need to keep us in trim and protect ourselves from

---

[12] See my article "Pierre Manent's *Montaigne*," *Perspectives on Political Science*, 45:4 (2016): 1–8.

the inconveniences that the other extreme, slack and sluggish idleness, brings in its train. (I.39.220)

Specifying what this attitude means for intellectual life, Montaigne writes: "as for plunging in deeper, or gnawing my nails over the study of Aristotle, monarch of modern learning, or stubbornly pursuing some part of knowledge, I have never done it" (I.26.129). Throughout the essays, Montaigne insists that he never takes anything too seriously: he reads, but only for entertainment; he travels, but with none of the exalted goals of the explorer or the pilgrim; he was mayor, but scrupulously avoided pouring his soul into politics: "the mayor and Montaigne have always been two, with a very clear separation" (III.10.941). Our souls, Montaigne teaches, "reach out beyond us;" we want to feel that our projects are larger than ourselves, that we can transcend ourselves by living up to a higher law, and it is thus that we enslave ourselves to the standard of a monstrous perfection (I.3.9). The soul's greatness, he tells us, "is exercised not in greatness, but in mediocrity" (III.2.745). Nonchalance is the Montaignean version of the traditional virtue of moderation; it teaches him to remain "at home," the heart of his conception of self-knowledge.

The second virtue of Montaignean naturalism is authenticity. To be clear, Montaigne does not use the word "authenticity," but it is a useful shorthand for the loyalty to what he calls our *forme maîtresse*— our individual, unchangeable "ruling pattern"—that he praises. "There is no one who, if he listens to himself, does not discover in himself a pattern of his own, a ruling pattern, which struggles against education and against the tempest of the passions that oppose it," he writes, and specifies that "my behavior is natural; I have not called in the help of any teaching to build it" (III.2.746; II.12.497). Montaignean authenticity is a loyalty to nature as opposed to teaching, to life in its movement as opposed to law in its fixity, to our particular individuality rather than general moral rules (III.13.1024, 1044). It entails becoming what one is, in Nietzsche's phrase.[13]

Montaigne manifests his authenticity in the way he presents himself relative to other human examples in the *Essays*. Montaigne's book abounds with meditations on the great souls of antiquity, but he does not model his life after them or anyone else. Indeed, as Pierre Manent points out, he declares at least three times that his judgment and his "universal opinions" have remained unaltered since childhood.[14] The experience of conversion, or even profound reform, in response to any moral example or teaching, is always an act of self-deception for Montaigne. He seeks rather to "loyally enjoy" his own being as given, and, at least according to him, succeeds: "If I had to live over again, I would live as I have lived. I have neither tears for the past nor fears about the future" (III.2.752). To be what one is, true to one's particular and distinctive nature, without regrets, is Montaignean authenticity.

The third virtue of Montaignean private life is frankness. Montaigne's frankness is famous, and he makes extraordinary claims for it: "I expose myself entire: my portrait is a cadaver on which the veins, the muscles, and the tendons appear at a glance, each part in its place.... It is not my deeds that I write down; it is myself; it is my essence" (II.6.332-333). Montaigne here claims an extraordinary degree of both self-knowledge and self-exposure to his reader; he vivisects himself. He juxtaposes this frankness to hypocrisy, which he puts at the head of the "ordinary vices" of his time:

> As for this new-fangled virtue of hypocrisy and dissimulation, which is so highly honored at present, I mortally hate it; and of all vices, I know none that testifies to so much cowardice and baseness of heart. It is a craven and servile idea to disguise ourselves and hide under a mask, and not to dare to show ourselves as we are. In that way our men train for perfidy; being accustomed to speak false

---

[13] Friedrich Nietzsche, *On the Genealogy of Morals and Ecce Homo*, ed. Walter Kauffman (New York: Vintage, 1967) 215.

[14] See Manent, *Montaigne: la vie sans loi* (Paris: Flammarion, 2014) 357n1, and *Essays* I.26.149, II.17.606, and II.2.748.

words, they have no scruples about breaking their word. (II.17.596)[15]

Montaigne claims to dissimulate nothing, hide nothing: "my face gives me away from the start" (III.13.1026). Some scholars have taken this frankness to be a kind of studied posture, even an elaborate, naturalistic mask.[16] Montaigne addresses this charge directly:

> Those who commonly contradict what I profess, saying that what I call frankness, simplicity, and naturalness in my conduct is art and subtlety, and rather prudence than goodness, artifice than nature, good sense than good luck, do me more honor than they take away from me. But surely they make my subtlety too subtle. And if anyone follows and watches me closely, I will concede him the victory if he does not confess that there is no rule in their school that could reproduce this natural movement and maintain a picture of liberty and license so constant and inflexible on such tortuous and varied paths, and that all their attention and ingenuity could not bring them to it. (III.1.731)

In the final analysis, only Montaigne himself could ever know how studied or unstudied his self-portrait actually was. The virtue he seeks to exemplify, however, is intelligible and familiar to us. Montaigne presents himself as a man who lays himself bare, as an exemplar of the unity of word and deed that can be achieved not by raising ourselves so as to live up to our promises and pretensions, but rather by measuring our speech against the reality of how we truly live.

Frankness is closely connected to the final Montaignean virtue, humanity. "A generous heart should not belie its thoughts," he writes, "it wants to reveal them even to its inmost depths. There everything is good, or at least everything is human" (II.17.596). Montaigne promises to frankly avow his full humanity. In this, we can see how Montaigne transmutes Christian virtues and practices. Outwardly Catholic from cradle to grave, Montaigne describes his book as his "confes-

---

[15] See also Judith N. Shklar, *Ordinary Vices* (Cambridge: Harvard University Press, 1985) and *Essays*, I.31.189.

[16] See Schaefer, *Political Philosophy of Montaigne*, chapter 1.

sion" (II.17.602). But it is a most novel kind of confession because Montaigne does not make his confession to a priest and he does not ask for forgiveness. Rather, he makes his confession to his reader, implicitly saying to us, as Pierre Manent has put it, "it is a human being I display to you, and you, too, are human."[17] That is, Montaigne asks us to receive his frank avowal of his full humanity with some humanity of our own.

In the *Essays*, Montaigne himself exemplifies this humanity by following Terence's famous maxim, "nothing human is foreign to me." His book displays his ability to enter sympathetically into almost every human posture—pagan or Christian, skeptical or superstitious, heroic or humble. He even suggests that Europeans have much to learn, morally speaking, from the naked, illiterate, heathen cannibals of the new world (I.31.189). It is all, after all, human nature.

In addition to being natural, all of these virtues are a- and even anti-political. Nothing could be more contrary to Machiavelli's self-transforming, fortune conquering ambition and glory-seeking—which readily employ hypocrisy and cruelty when those means are necessary—than Montaignean nonchalance, authenticity, frankness, and humanity. Montaigne does not seek to teach us how to scale the heights of power, persuade masses of men to follow us, or expand our empires. Rather, he seeks to teach us to be loyal to, honest about, and happy with the human condition. The virtues of such a life are private and moral rather than public and political.

Montaigne's anti-political account of virtue also reverses the classical and Christian understanding of human excellence. Rather than understanding law and politics as crucial to the pursuit of our natural human *telos*, Montaigne understands the quest to live naturally to entail a retreat from the political world. Politics and law thus become much more unnatural for Montaigne than they were for Plato, Aristotle, and Thomas Aquinas. Montaigne has reconceived nature. As a result, he must reconceive law in the light of his implicit

---

[17] Manent, *Montaigne*, 163.

denial of the traditional proposition that man is by nature a political animal.

Montaignean Moral Naturalism and the Rule of Law

Montaigne takes up the traditional distinction between nature and custom and radicalizes it, divorcing custom and nature altogether. Custom is merely custom: "laws remain in credit not because they are just, but because they are laws. That is the mystic foundation of their authority; they have no other" (III.13.1000). One of his favorite rhetorical maneuvers is to amass catalogs of contrary customs so as to reduce all human usages to a common level of arbitrariness. Reason cannot give a reason for the incest taboo, or a solid argument against cannibalism, or show that it is more sensible to worship the invisible God of the Bible than birds or snakes (I.23.96-100). Montaigne tells the story of his own attempt to discover the original justification of "one of our observances"—perhaps so as to defend some Catholic practice before the challenge of the Reformation, as Manent conjectures—only to find that "its foundation [was] so weak that I nearly became disgusted with it" (I.23.101).[18] The substance of law is and always will be arbitrary.

While the arbitrariness of law might seem to some a reason for revolution, Montaigne makes of it a reason for conservatism. He distinguishes four possible human attitudes toward law. The first is that of "simple peasants," who are "less curious and less learned," and who make "good Christians" and "honest men." These first and simplest of human types "believe simply and maintain themselves under the law;" they follow the laws in the belief that they are actually just. The second, decisive category is that of minds of "middling vigor," the "half-breeds" who have enough education to be arrogant and interpret the conservatism of the first type as "simplicity and stupidity." This type sees—rightly—the arbitrariness and injustice of the laws of their country, but fails to see the necessity for them. Caught with their "asses between two saddles," "these men trouble the world." Mon-

---

[18]Manent, *Montaigne*, 234.

taigne's third class is that of "great minds," who "by long and religious investigation, penetrate...the mysterious and divine secret of our Ecclesiastical polity"—*notre police ecclesiastique*, by which name he designates the whole political-theological order of his time. As for himself, Montaigne reports that he tried to escape the first state of ignorance but failed to reach the high enlightenment of great minds, and therefore, so as to get out of the world-troubling middle, retreated toward the "first and natural state" (I.54.275-276). He constitutes a fourth class, which, rather than seeking to reform the world or penetrate the "mysterious and divine secret" that makes sense of "our ecclesiastical polity," abandons the quest for just and rational laws and follows custom simply as custom. He thereby becomes as conservative as the first class of simple minds—indeed, more conservative than they—but ironically.[19]

Montaigne's ironic conservativism is the political consequence of his remodeled moral naturalism. Political law is pure convention; Montaigne follows the laws not because they are just but because they are laws, and because, as Erich Auerbach comments, he believes "there is no hope of finding [better ones] and the disorder involved in any change is a definite evil."[20] But this outward conservatism hardly enters into contact with the core of Montaigne's life: as he writes, "our laws are free enough, and the weight of sovereignty hardly touches a French gentleman two times in his life" (I.42.236). The substance of Montaigne's life is not to be found in the political world at all, but in the world of private life, where living naturally is possible. The world of law and politics is a world of artifice, more trouble to reform than to outwardly obey, while retaining an *arrière-boutique*, a back shop of the soul, in which our real mental and moral life occurs, unimpeded by arbitrary custom (I.39.214).

---

[19] In seeing Montaigne as conservative, even radically so, my view here coincides with the position Ann Hartle has articulated in her article "Montaigne's Radical Conservatism," *Modern Age*, 55: 4 (Fall 2013) 19-29.

[20] Erich Auerbach, *Scenes From the Drama of European Literature: Six Essays* (New York: Meridian Books, 1959) 104.

Conclusion: Montaigne, Machiavelli, and
the Problem of Modernity

Montaigne's ateleological, apolitical moral naturalism is the properly modern counterpoint to Machiavelli's hyper-political, Promethean anti-naturalism. The modern age oscillates between these two poles. This oscillation is nowhere clearer than the thought of Rousseau.[21] Rousseau follows the spirit of Montaigne in his *Second Discourse* and writes a devastating critique of politics and the arts self-consciously intended to encourage nostalgia for the pure state of nature. By contrast, in some of his other writings, Rousseau follows the spirit of Machiavelli in suggesting that the best social institutions are those that know how to most fully "denature man."[22] Moreover, as modern human beings, each of us probably has some experience of this oscillation in our lives: on the one hand, we delight in the Machiavellianism of cultural productions such as *House of Cards*, and the thrill of the successful maneuver in our professional and political dealings and doings. On the other, we hate politicians, and sometimes hate the political side of ourselves, and long to flee from both into the world of private life, where we can be our authentic selves, treat one another with humanity, and speak our minds frankly. Machiavellianism, after all, is brutal, isolating, and exhausting.

As such, Machiavellianism surely required the counterpoint of Montaigne's moral naturalism. As Manent points out, however much agreement there may be between Montaigne and Machiavelli about the problems created by the theologico-political tensions of their blood-soaked times, Montaigne "expects nothing of a Machiavellianism that, in short, aims to correct the vices of the time—dissimulation and cruelty—by the same vices."[23] As clear-eyed and clever as Machi-

---

[21] On oscillation in Rousseau, see Jonathan Marks, *Perfection and Disharmony in the Thought of Jean-Jacques Rousseau* (Cambridge: Cambridge University Press, 2005) 7, 52.

[22] Rousseau, *Emile*, trans. Allan Bloom (New York: Basic Books, 1979) 41.

[23] Manent, *Montaigne*, 217.

avelli plainly is, Montaigne would not be the last to think the Florentine, at bottom, a teacher of evil.

But one might wonder if, in his flight from Machiavellianism,
Montaigne does not incur the guilt of the same vices of which Machiavelli accuses the pious and the philosophers: of tacitly granting
criminals the right to dominate the human world by refusing to fight
it out in the rough and tumble struggle of politics. To be sure, Montaigne did not come by his assurance that we can abandon politics to
seek happiness in private life cheaply; a great deal of the charm of the
Essays resides in the hedonistic ebullience Montaigne cultivates in
some of the worst political circumstances imaginable, as the wars of
religion that were the context of his adult life swirled around the walls
of his chateau and sometimes came inside.[24] Nonetheless, one cannot
help but hear Machiavelli's warning that public life will not take care
of itself if good men hold themselves aloof from it.

Perhaps, then, a middle way is necessary between Montaigne
and Machiavelli, a way that accepts politics as an inescapable part of
human life without accepting the bellicose and radically amoral logic
of the Florentine. Perhaps that middle way—natural, political, and
moral at once—is to be found in a reconsideration of the classical and
Christian tradition both Machiavelli and Montaigne reject.

---

[24] Sarah Bakewell's *How To Live, or a life of Montaigne, in One Question and
Twenty Attempts at an Answer* (New York: Other Press, 2010) beautifully tells the
story of Montaigne's struggle to retain his humanity amid the political-
theological struggle of his time. See, in particular, chapters 12 and 15.

4

THE FOUNDATIONS OF LOCKE'S
DEFENSE OF POLITICAL TOLERATION
AND THE LIMITS OF REASON

Andrea Kowalchuk

Although Locke is frequently looked to in connection with the study of philosophical and political history, and his ideas about political toleration are widely acknowledged as foundational for America, today he is rarely taken seriously as an authority capable of influencing current debates about toleration and political morality. This is for two main reasons. First, Locke's arguments in defense of toleration are often dismissed because of their exclusivity: he explicitly argues against tolerating atheists and Catholics, and for most Americans, this is unacceptable. The second reason why we tend to ignore Locke's arguments today is that they have a distinctly religious character. Since America no longer considers itself a uniformly Christian nation, Christian arguments in favor of religious toleration are not sufficiently general as to command universal assent. If I am an atheist, why should I listen to Locke? Why should I be tolerant, especially when he is so clearly intolerant of me? Many people today and in recent history argue that what is currently necessary is a rational and secular defense of toleration, one that is tolerant of believers and non-believers alike, and wholly independent of any theological foundation, the assumption being that a secular argument is uniquely capable of the universalism sought.[1] If this is so, then Locke's arguments appear to be irrelevant to our goal.

---

[1] For an articulation of the "secularist objection" to a religious defense of toleration, see Susan Mendus, "Locke: Toleration, Morality, and Rationality," in *John Locke: A Letter Concerning Toleration in Focus*, eds. John Horton and Susan

I argue, against this view, that it is a mistake to disregard Locke's arguments, not because I think America should return to a state of narrower tolerance, and not because I think Locke's defense of toleration is strictly rational and secular, as some scholars argue. [2] Rather, I argue for Locke's continued relevance because I think his arguments raise politically and philosophically significant questions, and in so doing, they challenge current assumptions about the possibility of a rationalistic, secular, universal defense of toleration. What is especially interesting about Locke is that despite his rejection of a teleological and morally significant Nature, he nevertheless offers a robust defense of both morality and rational moral reasoning, and the particular defense he makes reveals what is, for him, the only possible ground. For Locke, there is no way to ground morality other than through a providential God who offers eternal rewards and punishments. Moreover, I argue, for Locke there is no way to defend the possibility of moral reasoning without such a God. Thus, what we

---

Mendus (London: Routledge, 1991) 148; Micah Schwartzman, "The Relevance of Locke's Religious Arguments for Toleration," *Political Theory* 33:5 (Oct. 2005): 678-705. See also John Dunn "What is Living and What is Dead in John Locke," in *Interpreting Political Responsibility* (Oxford: Polity Press, 1990) 12; Paul Bou-Habib, "Locke, Sincerity and the Rationality of Persecution," *Political Studies* 51 (2003): 611-12.

[2] For articulations of the view that Locke's political thought does not rest on theological foundations, see Thomas Pangle, *The Spirit of Modern Republicanism: The Moral Vision of the American Founders and the Philosophy of Locke* (Chicago and London: Chicago University Press, 1988); Michael P. Zuckert, "Locke: Religion: Equality", *Review of Politics*, 67:3 (Summer, 2005) 419-431. For articulations of the view that Locke's political thought does rest on theological foundations, see John Dunn, *The Political Thought of John Locke* (Cambridge: Cambridge University Press, 1969); Jeremy Waldron, *God, Locke and Equality: Christian Foundations of John Locke's Political Thought* (Cambridge: Cambridge University Press, 2002). David Wootton suggests that Locke, a Socian, grounded his thought in theology but continued to hope that the law of nature could in fact be demonstrated despite the fact that he himself never succeeded in doing so. See David Wootton, "John Locke: Socian or Natural Law Theorist?" in *Religion, Secularization and Political Thought: Thomas Hobbes to J.S. Mill,* ed. James E. Crimmins (London and New York: Routledge, 1990) 39-67, and Steven Forde, *Locke, Science and Politics* (Cambridge: Cambridge University Press, 2014).

learn from his defense is what Locke thinks must be true in order to make a persuasive case for the moral life and in order to ground the possibility of human moral knowledge. His conclusions, I argue, rule out the possibility of the rational, secular, universal defense of toleration sought, and in some cases assumed, today.

Locke's Defense of Toleration in the *Letter*

Locke's defense of toleration in the *Letter Concerning Toleration*[3] depends on roughly four kinds of arguments: prudential or pragmatic arguments, arguments that appeal to emotion, epistemological arguments, or those having to do with the limits of knowledge, and finally, theological arguments, including those rooted in scripture. Before considering why, from Locke's perspective, a compelling rational secular argument for toleration is impossible, it is helpful to say a little more about each type of claim. The first class of argument Locke uses is a prudential or pragmatic argument, which has to do with political necessity. Such arguments are rooted in observations about the way men necessarily behave, and conclude with commands about how to avoid undesirable behavior or outcomes. For example, Locke argues that revolution is the predictable consequence of oppression, since men subjected to onerous burdens will necessarily attempt to rid themselves of them:

> Oppression raises Ferments, and makes men struggle to cast off an uneasie and tyrannical Yoke. I know that Seditions are very frequently raised, upon pretense of Religion. But 'tis as true that, for Religion, Subjects are often ill-treated, and live miserably. Believe me, the Stirs that are made, proceed not from any peculiar temper of this or that Church or Religious Society; but from the common Disposition of all Mankind, who when they groan under any heavy burden, endeavor naturally to shake off the Yoke that galls their neck. (52)

---

[3] John Locke, *A Letter Concerning Toleration*, ed. James H. Tully (Indianapolis: Hackett Publishing Co, 1983).

Although Locke here acknowledges that religion is often used as a pretense for such revolutions or rebellions, and thus, that intolerance is not the sole source of unrest, his point is that when religious persecution does occur, it leads naturally to rebellion. And in fact, it occurs so often that Locke feels comfortable suggesting it is the primary if not sole cause of religious conflict in the Christian world: "It is not the diversity of Opinions, (which cannot be avoided) but the refusal of Toleration to those that are of Different Opinions, (which might have been granted) that has produced all the Bustles and Wars, that have been in the Christian world, upon account of Religion" (55). Locke's argument in sum: men go to war due to intolerance; war is undesirable; therefore, be tolerant.

The second kind of argument that Locke makes in the *Letter* is what I refer to as an emotional argument. He frequently enjoins his reader to be tolerant, not just of other Christians, but of people of diverse beliefs, including Muslims, pagans, and American Indians. In these instances, Locke uses a combination of theological and prudential arguments, but they are often supplemented with an appeal to the feelings of the reader. In effect, Locke asks how the reader would feel were he subject to oppression at the hands of these different groups (40, 43). The intended effect is to arouse the sympathies of the reader, in addition to effacing the differences between men.

In addition to making appeals to our sympathies and to arguing that religious toleration is politically expedient, Locke argues that the duty of tolerance follows from the fact that human understanding is limited, and cannot, on its own, discern the truth about this or that religion. This third kind of argument could be termed an epistemological argument, one rooted in an articulation of the limits of reason or the nature of human understanding. Locke says of the multitude of Christian denominations, for example, that "[t]here is only one of these (sects of Christianity) which is the true way to Eternal Happiness. But in this great variety of ways that men follow, it is still doubted which is the right one" (36). He also suggests that because the nature of the understanding is to give way, not to force, but to "light and evidence," it is futile to try and compel men to believe specific doctrines (27). From these two premises—that human understanding is limited, and that no man can be compelled to believe anything by force—Locke concludes that 1) "the care of man's soul belongs to himself" (35) and 2) because every church is "orthodox to itself," no single church can impose its views on men. For Locke, only the Supreme judge of man can decide between the various religions (32).

The final type of argument that Locke makes in the *Letter* is an argument rooted in scriptural interpretation. Key examples of such arguments are: "Toleration [is] the chief characteristical mark of the true church... *The Kings of the Gentiles exercise Lordship over them*, said our Savior to his disciples, *but ye shall not be so* (Luke 22, 25)" (23); "there is no evidence in the Bible to suggest Christians should persecute others" (29-30); "Jews fell into idolatry by following kings" (37); "Follow Christ's method: he was the prince of peace" (25); "It is more agreeable to the true church to focus on what Jesus said, not on external doctrine" (29). These and other doctrines are rooted in scripture, and from these doctrines, it follows that:

1. There is no obligation to convert sinners by force; all conversion must happen through persuasion.
2. Anyone who seeks power does so from love of dominion, not concern for men's souls.
3. The true church is not involved in political affairs.
4. Laity and believers have a duty to seek peace.
5. Laity and believers all have a duty to promote toleration.

Locke's often heterodox interpretation of scripture raises the crucial question of whether it is reason or revelation that has final authority for him. Moreover, the fact that Locke offers multiple arguments has led many scholars to ask whether they are mutually dependent, separable, or even whether one type is insincere or merely a screen.[4] Although some of these questions will be taken up below, for the moment it is sufficient to note that Locke's theological arguments have authority because they are rooted in scripture; this is what makes them different than the non-theological arguments appealing to necessity. They are important for two key reasons: first, religious readers would not have accepted strictly pragmatic arguments, and second, for Locke a defense of morality is impossible without an ultimate appeal to Providence.

The Relevance of Locke's Scriptural Arguments: Is a Purely Rational, Secular Defense of Toleration and Morality *Universal?*

As I noted above, some scholars argue that what is required today is a purely rational, secular defense of toleration, and for this reason Locke is a problematic authority; after all, many of his arguments are not only theological in character, but specifically Christian. Whether a strictly rational, secular argument could achieve the kind of universality sought, however, is an open question. In order to see the possible difficulty of securing assent to such an argument more clearly, consider the implications of removing all of Locke's arguments that are rooted in scripture and/or theology. We would be left with prudential, emotional, and epistemological arguments. Would these arguments be sufficient on their own to win the support of a serious believer?

---

[4]For versions of the argument that Locke's theological arguments are insincere and intended to protect him from persecution see Leo Strauss, *Natural Right and History* (University of Chicago Press, 1953) 212-14, 227-29; Leo Strauss "Locke's Doctrine of Natural Law," reprinted in *What is Political Philosophy? And Other Studies* (Westport, CT: Greenwood Press, 1959) 201-6; Thomas Pangle, *The Spirit of Modern Republicanism: The Moral Vision of the American Founders and the Philosophy of Locke*, 136-60, 196-211; Michael Zuckert, *Natural Rights and the New Republicanism* (Princeton University Press, 1998) 237-240, 274. Against this view, Steven Forde argues that Locke is forced to appeal to God as a consequence of his rejection of a teleological universe, and that this appeal is not merely a screen. See Forde, *Locke, Science and Politics*, 104-8.

The short answer to this question is no, but to understand why, let us consider a wider context. In order to make a case for toleration, Locke must admit that human understanding is limited. This is key if he is to convince people that no specific religion ought to assert itself as the only true religion. But no sooner does he admit this than a difficulty arises. If it is true that no man knows the final truth when it comes to religion, then how could, or why why should a serious believer accept rational arguments about toleration at all? This is tough for us to see now because we are so committed to the sanctity of toleration, but why wouldn't a serious believer want to live in a political community that supports and reinforces the religious laws and customs she values? Here John Winthrop is instructive:

> the end is to improve our lives to do more service to the Lord; the comfort and increase of the body of Christ, whereof we are members, that ourselves and posterity may be the better preserved from the common corruptions of this evil world, to serve the Lord and work out our salvation under the power and purity of his holy ordinances. [5]

As Winthrop's words reflect, believers may desire to live in a community that reflects and promotes, even mandates, the religious aspirations of the group. For a serious believer who longs for a political community that protects and promotes what he see as his God-given duties, it will take more than an argument concerning what is politically pragmatic to convince him to become tolerant of other ways of life. From the believer's perspective, arguments about what is politically expedient often will not outweigh concerns about the duties of one's soul, and one's fate in the afterlife.

Locke understood this. Accordingly, he had to show that Christianity was itself compatible with what he was proposing. He had to show, using scripture itself, that toleration was a Christian duty. If Locke admits that reason is limited, how could he ever expect to convince a serious believer to do something that contradicts her faith?

---

[5] John Winthrop, *A Model of Christian Charity*, 1630 (http://history.hanover.edu/texts/winthmod.html).

Locke understood that a purely secular defense of toleration is not as universal as we today tend to think, and therefore that scriptural arguments were relevant and even necessary to his end.

The Relevance of Locke's Scriptural Arguments: Is a Purely Rational, Secular Defense of Toleration and Morality *Possible?*

For Locke, a rational, secular defense of morality cannot hope to win universal assent. But this raises a set of further and deeper questions: is a religious or theological defense of toleration necessary for merely practical reasons—because a secular rationalistic argument would not be accepted by believers? Or is such an argument inadequate or even impossible according to the standards of reason itself?

Towards the end of the *Letter,* Locke offers what seems to be a pretty clear answer to this question:

> Those are not to be tolerated who deny the Being of God. Promis-
> es, Covenants, and Oaths, which are the bonds of Humane Society,
> can have no hold upon an atheist. The taking away of God, tho but
> even in thought, dissolves all. Besides also, those that by their
> Atheism undermine and destroy all religion, can have no pretense
> of Religion whereupon to challenge the Privilege of a Toleration.
> (51)

Despite the clarity of Locke's statement in this text, he offers very little by way of supportive reasoning other than to emphasize the impossibility of oaths and promises for one who does not believe in God. If the argument is going to be more than merely pragmatic, it is necessary to move beyond the *Letter* to seek his support for the claim. The first text we will consult is *The Reasonableness of Christianity,* which is the text so often used to defend the claim that Locke ultimately abandoned his hope that reason could ground morality, and where we will examine Locke's reasons for looking to God as the foundation of morality. It is in this text that we see Locke's most robust defense of revelation as the true moral guide for man's actions. Some argue that the *Reasonableness* reflects Locke's mature view, a significant departure from his original optimism about reason. That earlier, more optimistic, position is said to be reflected in *The Essay Concerning Human Understanding*, where Locke argues for a purely rational kind of moral certitude.[6] But as Forde suggests, Locke continued to edit the *Essay* at the same time that he was writing *The Reasonableness of Christianity*, which implies greater compatibility between the two texts than is often admitted.[7] We will look to the *Essay* to examine precisely how optimistic Locke was about the possibility of a rational defense of morality.[8] Specifically, we will consider Locke's understanding of the necessary connection between God and the possibility of moral reasoning. I will conclude that Locke's defense of rational morality is in fact much more qualified than some commentators admit. On my view, Locke was always keenly aware of the necessity for a theological defense of morality, and never believed in the possibility of a binding rational, secular defense of morality in general, and of toleration in particular.

The Ground of Morality in *The Reasonableness of Christianity*

In *The Reasonableness of Christianity*, Locke devotes considerable attention to the question of whether or not reason can reach the same conclusions as those revealed by the Christian Bible.[9] He indicates

---

[6] See Richard Ashcraft, "Faith and Knowledge in Locke's Philosophy", in *John Locke: Problems and Perspectives*, ed. John Yolton (Cambridge University Press, 1969) 194-223; Dunn, *The Political Thought of John Locke*, 18, 198.

[7] See Steven Forde, "Natural Law, Theology, and Morality in Locke," *American Journal of Political Science* 45:2 (2001): 405-8; Forde, *Locke, Science and Morality*, 193-4.

[8] See footnote 2 and 4 above. Zuckert argues that Locke depends on reason, not revelation, to arrive at his defense of morality, though he also admits that reason leads Locke to a natural theology. See Zuckert, "Locke: Equality: Religion," 424-6, 430-31. Ultimately, Zuckert looks to Locke for guidance to a wholly rational defense of liberal principles. See Zuckert, *New Republicanism*, 277-78, 286. I differ from these scholars in my view that Locke was much more interested in and concerned with the limits of reason than their studies admit.

[9] All references are to John Locke, *The Reasonableness of Christianity with A Discourse of Miracles and Part of A Third Letter Concerning Toleration*, ed. I.T.

that some elements of that teaching can be reached by unaided human reason. The pagans, he explains, will not all be punished because some of them understood parts of what he calls "the Law of Works," which consists of two components: general moral teachings accessible through a God-given conscience, and the specific laws detailed to the Jews. Because pagans understand the general moral teachings of this Law, it seems Locke assigns a fairly robust role to reason, and has confidence in the possibility of genuine moral knowledge. Locke frequently confirms this suggestion throughout the *Essay*, as he discusses the early and ancient moral philosophers and emphasizes their significant contributions to ethics. At times he states plainly that reason can, in principle, deduce the moral law, but that the task is difficult, and has simply not been fulfilled. But when Locke considers directly the challenge of deducing the moral law, the question arises as to whether reason can, in fact, ground moral knowledge.

The first difficulty Locke mentions has to do with the second component of the Law of Works. The Law of Works consists, not just in general moral principles, which Locke equates with the law of nature, and refers to as the moral law (19), but in a very specific list of laws detailed to the Jews, all of which, according to Locke, Jesus acknowledges and requires of man (18, 188). Human reason would therefore have to prove capable of deducing from certain principles obligations like the necessity of compassion, loving one's enemy, and others.[10] But Locke admits such a list has never been articulated outside the Christian tradition and its influence:

> Experience shows, that the knowledge of morality, by mere natural light, (how agreeable soever it be to it,) makes but a slow progress, and little advance in the world. And the reason of it is not hard to be found in men's necessities, passions, vices, and mistaken interests; which turn their thoughts another way...Or whatever else was

---

Ramsay (Stanford: Stanford University Press, 1958) and *An Essay Concerning Human Understanding* (Amherst: Prometheus Books, 1995).

[10] Locke details a long list of moral duties identified by Jesus in his Sermon on the Mount, which Locke associates with the moral law, the part of the Law of Works discernable by reason (188).

> the cause, it is plain, in fact, that human reason unassisted failed
> men in its great and proper business of morality. It never from un-
> questionable principles, by clear deductions, made out an entire
> body of the "law of nature." And he that shall collect all the moral
> rules of the philosophers, and compare them with those contained
> in the New Testament, will find them to come short of the morality
> delivered by our Saviour, and taught by his apostles; a college made
> up, for the most part, of ignorant, but inspired fishermen (86).

The difficulty of providing such a detailed account of the law of nature is formidable. In this passage Locke points a finger at necessity,
vice, and passion, from which we can infer a tension between what
men might be required to do given the demands of compassion or
charity, on the one hand, and what they might prefer to do given
their needs, passions and vices, on the other. Should I be starving and
poor, for example, or even greedy and gluttonous, the necessity of
charity would appear to be extremely difficult to defend from the perspective of unaided human reason. This is so in large part because for
Locke, all men do and must seek pleasure—there is no alternative end
which we pursue (*Essay* II.21.41; 62). The very fact that compassion
and liberality are duties indicates that they are not self-evidently good
for us, at least in the sense that they are not self-evidently more pleasant than providing for ourselves either to meet necessity or to satisfy a
passion. At this point in *The Reasonableness of Christianity*, Locke
gives no indication of how pleasure is to be reconciled or harmonized
with duty. The tension we here infer leads us to a deep problem that
Locke soon acknowledges in the text: no one, prior to Biblical Revelation, he explains, ever established the existence of a genuine human
duty to be good.

> He that any one will pretend to set up in this kind, and have his
> rules pass for authentic directions, must shew, that either he builds
> his doctrines upon principles of reason, self-evident in themselves,
> and that he deduces all the parts of it from thence, by clear and evi-
> dent demonstration; or he must shew his commission from heav-
> en...In the former way, *nobody that I know, before our Savior's time*

77

ever did, or went about to give us a morality. Tis true, there is a law of nature: but…who ever made out all of the parts of it together, and shewed the world their obligation? (242, my emphasis)

If someone is to fully discover the law of nature by means other than revelation, he must discover self-evident principles from which he can deduce all the particular laws by clear and evident demonstration. He must also prove, presumably in so doing, that man is *obliged* to follow those laws. Importantly, says Locke, a duty cannot be grounded successfully in pragmatic arguments:

> The rules of morality were, in different countries and sects, different. And natural reason no where had, nor was like to cure the defects in them. Those just measures of right and wrong, which necessity had anywhere introduced, the civil laws prescribed, or philosophy recommended, stood not on their true foundations. They were looked on as bonds of society, and conveniences of common life, and laudable practices. But where was it their obligation was thoroughly known and allowed, and they received as precepts of law, of the highest law, of the law of nature? *That could not be, without a clear knowledge and acknowledgment of the law-maker, and the great rewards and punishments, for those who would or would not obey him.* (243, my emphasis)

For Locke, it is not enough that the demands of virtue be anchored in utility or perceived honorability. They must be shown to command a duty. Pagan philosophers had hitherto failed to do so because they had failed to demonstrate the existence of God, and not just any God, but a providential God. For Locke, an abstract principle, or "philosopher's God," which orders the cosmos, is not a viable alternative to a providential God. In the *Essay*, Locke vaguely references this theological cosmic view by stating that the closest ancient philosophers came to convincing man of the goodness of virtue was by positing a human nature and a perfection. These claims are of a piece with the old philosophical system which relied on essences and ideas, which Locke explicitly rejects in the *Essay*.[11] Nature, for Locke, is void of moral content, which means that moral grounds *have* to be discovered in some alternative. For Locke, that alternative is God, a being separate and distinct from Nature.

In addition, the divine lawgiver must be shown to reward virtue and punish vice, and for this to be possible, there must be an afterlife that corrects for the unpleasantness of the virtuous life in this world (161). Until Christ, no philosopher had successfully established a link between duty and happiness (88-89). Wherever an afterlife was discussed, says Locke, it was not taken seriously. As a result, duty and virtue were linked to political necessity or the conveniences of life and nobility, but could never bind a man, for a man will and ought to pursue his happiness.

Despite the difficulties of overcoming these challenges, and establishing morality on its true foundations, Locke continues to hold open the possibility that reason can discover all that is necessary in order to do so. He warns, however, against supposing that this grounding has already happened. It is very easy, once something has been introduced into common knowledge, in this case, through revelation, to believe that reason discovers what it in fact only confirms (86). The conclusions of the work are, therefore, that 1) the moral law, part of the Law of Works, is accessible to human reason; 2) never before has man discovered the law in its full detail; 3) if man were to discover it, its discovery would *presuppose* the discovery of a Providential God who is the necessary condition for the law. This last point is crucial because it indicates that for Locke, no defense of morality is possible without a God to reward and punish moral behavior. This means that no rational, secular defense of morality is possible. This point is repeated throughout the *Essay*, where Locke is at his most confident with respect to the power of reason. But what is also revealed, but ignored in scholarship, is that in the *Essay*, it is clear that not only does morality depend on the existence of a Providential God,

---

[11] For an excellent account of this rejection, see Forde, *Locke, Science, and Morality*, 14-71.

but so too does the very possibility of certitude in moral reasoning that Locke is so famous for asserting. That is, if we are to trust the conclusions of reason, there must be a God who designed man to have access to moral knowledge. Without such a God, our moral reasoning would be as uncertain as our empirical knowledge.

The Ground of Morality in the *Essay Concerning Human Understanding*

In the *Essay Concerning Human Understanding*, Locke famously rejects innate ideas and essences and the teleological cosmos on which they depend. With this rejection, the natural world becomes amoral. We can no longer look to Nature for a normative understanding of human behavior. As a consequence of this rejection, Locke is compelled to discover a new ground for moral knowledge, and this he found in a providential God. In *The Reasonableness of Christianity* Locke emphasizes the role of revelation in the discovery of a provident God, whereas in the *Essay* he emphasizes no such external need. In fact, Locke argues that man is capable of demonstrating, not only God's existence, but all of the moral laws that follow from God's existence. Indeed, for Locke, moral knowledge can be given in precise formulations akin to mathematics. What is crucial to understand, however, is that for Locke's claims about the certainty of moral knowledge to be true, it is *necessary* that God exists. Without a God, even the moral knowledge that appears free from the troubles that plague empirical inquiry will itself be subject to skepticism, in part because it too builds on sense perception, in part because it is subject to deeper limits. Those limits, which Locke acknowledges, have to do with the limits of human reason itself, and the purpose for which knowledge itself exists, which is survival, not contemplation. In this section, I will explain these limits with the goal of illuminating the reasons why, for Locke, a universal, rational, secular defense of morality and toleration is impossible.

As noted, in the *Essay*, Locke explicitly states that man can have certain moral knowledge, and that this knowledge comes from reason alone. Essential to his argument is the separation of two fundamental categories of knowledge. On the one hand, man seeks knowledge about the natural world, and on the other, he seeks moral knowledge. These two categories differ primarily with respect to their dependency on, or independence of, external data and sense experience. Whereas natural science examines the empirical world, and does so by means of imperfect senses, moral science, like mathematics, provides proofs by demonstrating agreement or disagreement between ideas that exist only in the mind. This division gives the impression that the sole cognitive or epistemological limit on inquiry is sense related, and that because moral knowledge is independent of both, it is unobstructed. But this is a false impression. The problems that pertain to natural science, those anchored in sense experience, ultimately do impact moral knowledge. Moreover, while it is true that much of Locke's consideration of the limits of mind focuses on issues or difficulties related to the senses, his deepest reservations concern the fundamental limits of reason itself, limits pertaining not only to the possibility of natural science, but also of moral knowledge.

In order to understand the cognitive limits to human inquiry, it is helpful to turn to Book IV of the *Essay*, where Locke explains many of these limits in the context of discussing human knowledge. For Locke, knowledge is the perception of agreement or disagreement between ideas in the mind, and we can have knowledge in varying degrees. Locke describes intuition, the clearest and most certain kind of knowledge, upon which all knowledge depends, as immediate recognition. When we grasp that one thing is not another, as red is distinct from blue, we do so without the help of any intervening ideas. Demonstration, a second category, entails immediate recognition, but is only achieved after intervening ideas or steps have been supplied to show how ideas either agree or disagree with each other. When we perceive such agreement or disagreement between ideas in the mind, we do so in one of four ways. We may recognize 1) identity, that x is not y, or red is not blue. We may recognize 2) the relations between ideas, as when we recognize that the three angles of a triangle are equal to two right angles. When we perceive agreement or disagreement with respect to co-existence, we recognize 3) the necessary connection between a set of qualities, as when the quality of being unconsumed in the fire always appears with certain qualities of yellowness and weight in gold, for example. And when we perceive 4) real existence, we do so intuitively, as with ourselves, or by way of demonstration, as with God, or by way of sensitive knowledge, as with all things currently sensible to us. Though each of these ways of knowing contributes to human knowledge, for Locke, each also entails serious limitations.

One of the most serious limitations Locke identifies pertains to the category of co-existence. Despite experiences and trials that seem to indicate that certain secondary qualities, like the quality of remaining unconsumed in fire together with a certain sort of yellowness and weight, constantly recur together, we cannot establish a necessary connection between such secondary qualities. We cannot do so because we cannot first establish a necessary connection between such secondary qualities and their primary qualities, and we cannot establish this more fundamental connection because we do not know the constitution of the minute particles on which such qualities depend. Our lack of knowledge about such minute particles also compromises our ability to know the specific powers of different substances, both active and passive—how the quality of yellow is able to affect our senses, for example. Although experience suggests that five qualities will constantly recur together in gold, we cannot demonstrate that connection by means of proofs that show entailment between these ideas. We therefore remain dependent on sense experience to observe such co-existence, and as a result, we cannot know for certain that the fifth quality will in fact show up with the other four. This is, of course, where probability factors into Locke's thinking about the natural world.

Another set of serious and intimately related limitations that Locke discusses have to do with the remoteness and minuteness of the substances around us. Because we cannot perceive and interact with most of what exists in the world, we lack ideas for most substances, and as a result, lack knowledge of them. Because we cannot identify those things which are remote, we cannot understand their secondary and primary qualities, nor can we understand their powers. This becomes especially clear when Locke speaks of the minute things. As explained above, for Locke, knowledge of co-existence and relation requires and even depends upon knowledge of the primary qualities that are beyond the scope of human faculties. Even if human beings could see the smallest of things, simple ideas corresponding to them would be insufficient to provide knowledge of co-existence and relation, since we would have to be able to establish reasoned accounts and universal principles that extended beyond experience and observation.

These problems are serious, but they are all problems pertaining to sense perception, and although Locke does not hold out vague promises of improved instruments designed to overcome such difficulties, it is not hard to imagine such hopes. However, in Book IV, Locke acknowledges a number of difficulties that far exceed those discussed above because they pertain not only to the imperfections of sense, but also imperfections or flaws with reason itself, at least with respect to its capacity to make sense of and understand fully the world taken in through experience. Locke is clear, for example, that our failure to understand matter is a significant obstacle to all of our knowledge. We cannot understand matter because it is beyond our senses, and it is beyond our senses, according to Locke, because our senses are not 'calibrated' to disinterestedly take in and process objective and complete data for the sake of contemplating truth. Rather, our senses are designed to help us with the demands of survival. If in fact our senses were designed to perceive the truth of things, man would have a very difficult time surviving. He would see the minute particles that make up beings, but not the beings themselves. Needless to say, this would compromise man's ability, not only to fend off beasts, but even to feed himself. Because sense data serves mainly the purpose of survival and not contemplation, man does not see what is unnecessary to that end (2.23.12; 3.30.2).[12] Other creatures may have better or more numerous senses, and higher creatures would have more intuitive knowledge than man. The very fact that man has to labor to understand his world and himself points to his cognitive limitations. Indeed, the design of man's non-contemplative mind makes it impossible to answer the most comprehensive and significant questions. Within the context of discussing the extent and limits of human knowledge, Locke indicates that some things are simply beyond the reach of human comprehension, and points to one such significant question or problem that may permanently escape man.

Man cannot know, says Locke, how thinking and matter relate to one another. This is because every possible answer that we can provide to the question turns out to be deeply problematic. If we consider the possibility that matter itself thinks, we run into an obstacle in our attempts to perceive or explain what would have to be true about the universe for this to follow. If matter thinks, then all that exists is matter. This would mean that matter would have to be the "eternal first thinking being," which Locke says is a contradiction, since matter is "void of sense and thought" (4.3.6). Presumably what he means is that matter, by definition, differs from beings that are alive and sensitive and perceptive. If we eliminate any non-material principles, it is very difficult to account for this perceptible difference and for the way we experience the world. According to our experience, it appears that living, thinking beings differ from non-thinking, material beings. If all that exists is material, there is no way to explain this difference, except perhaps, to explain it away. Despite our inability to do more than just state this alternative, that is, despite our inability to really *understand* this alternative, for Locke, it cannot be ruled out. Nor can

---

[12] In this general respect, then, Locke is a forefather of the epistemological position taken by thinkers such as Noam Chomsky, Colin McGinn, Jerry Fodor, and Gunther Stent, all of whom argue for some version of "cognitive closure," which claims that the mind, because of its natural history and consequent design structure, is simply unable to grasp certain features of reality. As a result, we are unlikely to answer definitively certain perennial questions in science and philosophy, like the mind-body problem.

the alternatives, if we are honest with ourselves about what we know, he cautions (4.3.6). We might also try positing a non-material substance to account for thought, but then we merely provide an unintelligible "place-holder" concept. It is and must be unintelligible because human beings cannot comprehend motion except in connection with physical contact.[13]

Locke's preferred hypothesis is that a God made material that thinks. This solves the problem that attends a strictly material account, while being compatible with his rejection of essences and teleological principles. But even when choosing sides, Locke is clear: without revelation, man will be forever incapable of knowing whether material is capable of thinking, or whether the power is joined to matter through some immaterial substance. Neither option, he warns, is more absurd than the other; each is equally unintelligible and equally likely to drive a man to the alternative view if he does not guard against zealotry. Locke's advice is to be honest with yourself about the extent to which this problem is beyond our reach.

This section of the *Essay* points to the limits of the human mind, not just because our senses are limited, but because certain problems evade intelligibility, like action at a distance, for example. We can infer, therefore, that whatever happens to be true about the universe, it is beyond man's ability to know—in general because we were not designed to contemplate or understand, and because reason seems to work in a restrictive way. We are simply incapable of understanding certain things. In light of the limitations of mind, then, what are we to make of Locke's claims that we can have certain *moral* knowledge? Does moral knowledge escape the problem of cognitive limits?

Math and moral knowledge are, for Locke, akin to science. They consist of proofs or chains of reasoning that explicate agreement and disagreement between different modes, or ideas in our minds, with no

---

[13] This is why Locke and so many others found Newton's discovery of gravity so deflating with respect to our ability to understand the world. For an excellent account of reactions to Newton, as well as Newton's himself, see Noam Chomsky, "The Mysteries of Nature: How Deeply Hidden", *The Journal of Philosophy*, Vol. CVI, No. 4 (April 2009): 167-200.

necessary referent outside themselves, and in so doing they secure something akin to intuitive knowledge through proofs (4.1-7). This is apparently what makes math and moral knowledge so reliable: they do nothing but explicate relations between "modes" and are independent of the empirical world. Locke emphasizes this point when he explains that there is no guarantee or necessity that pure mathematics or mixed modes correspond to the real world (2.22.2; 2.31.3; 3.5.3; 2.3.1-2; 2.22.8). If these forms of knowledge were not separate from the empirical world, they would not be certain. The purity and coherence of mathematical and moral reasoning are therefore set apart in Locke's analysis, and in being set apart appear to escape the limits that Locke articulates in connection with empirical data and study. However, when seen in light of the problems articulated above, it becomes clear that even moral knowledge is less certain than Locke would have us believe.

As a number of scholars have noticed, the mixed ideas that form the content of moral knowledge are themselves built up from simple ideas, which are wholly dependent on sense data. This would indicate that moral knowledge, being itself dependent on sense data, is subject to error in its assumptions, especially those that form the basis of definitions and ideas about what things are. If we must first know what man is in order to know what laws he is subject to, yet we can never know with certainty what man is (because we have no innate ideas or access to anything like an 'essence' for man), then any laws deduced from his nature would themselves be subject to error.[14] We could never know conclusively, for example, that man is "an understanding rational being" as Locke claims he is (4.3.18; see also 4.13.3). In fact, isn't man's understanding precisely what is in question? If the mind seeks useful knowledge rather than truth, isn't it at least possible, as so many contemporary thinkers argue, that morality comes into being

---

[14] See Waldron, *Locke, God, Equality*, 54-59; Lee Ward, "The Problematic Relationship Between Locke's Natural Science and Moral Philosophy" in *Matter and Form: From Natural Science to Political Philosophy*, ed. Ann Ward (Plymouth: Lexington Press, 2009) 179-194, especially 181-3; Forde, *Locke, Science and Politics*, 81-86.

to serve preservation, rather than as an accurate guide for our nature? Because Locke relies on definitions that are rooted in empirical data, his claim that the proof of our nature and the existence of God are sufficient to deduce the moral law is highly problematic. A man might be convinced of his moral knowledge and live accordingly, wholly unaware of the fact that his moral knowledge is the product of his own way of thinking, not an accurate reflection of what he is and how a being such as he is ought to behave. To restate this point, if all that exists is material, a possibility that Locke considered seriously, then moral knowledge would be the product of the way the human mind works, not the fruit of God's design. For Locke's moral knowledge to be certain, the mind *must* have been created by a providential God.

This is, of course, what Locke argues: God made man so that he knows what he needs to know. We can be certain of our moral certainty. If Locke did not point to a God who designed man this way, while also giving him sufficient abilities to come to Him and His law through reason, then man's moral reasoning would be subject to the same flaws to which his empirical reasoning is subject. Without a God, man's ability to know *anything* with accuracy would falter toward extreme skepticism. Because Locke points to such a God, and even claims that his existence can be demonstrated, he appears to escape such skepticism. But as he makes clear throughout his works, he himself proved incapable of making God's existence apodictically certain, as did any other human being who had tried to that point.[15]

Even if we were to accept Locke's argument about the possibility of moral knowledge, still, as Forde notes, this would not provide empirical proof of a God.[16] If we return to Locke's reflections on think-

---

[15] Locke was asked several times for such a proof. See Locke's replies to his friends, Molyneux, in his letters to him of September 20, 1692, January 19, 1694, and March 30, 1696 (http://oll.libertyfund.org.php?option+com_staticxt& staticfile=show.php%3Ftitle=1444&layout=html#chapter_81479) and to James Tyrell in *The Correspondence of John Locke*, 8 vols. Ed. E.S. de Beer (Oxford University Press, 1976) IV:101, 110-3.

[16] Forde, *Locke, Science and Morality*, 112-115.

ing matter, we can infer that Locke did, however, think he had probabilistic knowledge of God. Recall, Locke thinks that it is problematic to posit a strictly material universe because of the difficulty of understanding the existence of thinking matter. Though he considers the possibility, he does not find it convincing to posit eternal thinking matter. This means he has to posit some other being or principle, but since he has rejected innate ideas and essences, he has rejected the possibility of a teleological universe. The only other alternative is to posit a God, and though this may not be Locke's sole reason for taking this step, it is likely one of two major concerns that drove him to his conclusions, the other being, of course, that it is impossible to ground moral duty without a God. Regardless of whether Locke's arguments are compelling to his readers, especially current readers, their significance must be acknowledged. At the very least, we must recognize that Locke articulates forcefully why positing God makes rational sense if one wants to defend the possibility of moral duty in a non-teleological universe.

Conclusion

Whether Locke was a believer, or whether he was led to posit a God by his theoretical insights, is uncertain. Whether or not Locke saw all of the implications of the limits he discussed is also difficult to prove with certainty, as the extremely wide-ranging interpretations of Locke's intention and teachings show. Even if he did not see the full implications of his discussion of matter and the mind's limits, however, the problems remain: epistemological and cognitive limits to human knowledge suggest that a universal secular morality is nondefensible. Even Locke's certainty that God is necessary to ground moral duty, considered apart from the question of whether He in fact exists, is instructive with respect to these hopes. What Locke shows is that in order to preserve a firmly grounded morality in the absence of a teleological universe, one needs something like God, whether arrived at through reason or revelation. Granted, a simply pragmatic defense of morality is always possible, but as considered above, it cannot be fully convincing to believers. Moreover and I think more importantly, pragmatic moral arguments cannot be fully binding—that is, they cannot ground a duty, as Locke argues in *The Reasonableness of Christianity*.

Because the protection of rights is such a crucial component of American Republicanism, and the protection of rights nearly inconceivable without toleration, Locke's argument about the necessary foundations of morality in general, and toleration in particular, ought to be understood before it is set aside. The fact that morality may not be fully defensible on rational grounds may not sound altogether problematic or alarming in an age where values are routinely spoken of as relative, and perhaps, in some respects, there is nothing here to fear. But lest we accept with ease these implications before having seen them clearly for what they are, reference to specific examples is helpful. If there is no ground for morality, this means that even the most sacred principles of American political life should be subject to prudential considerations. Thus, even human rights would lack the universal and unquestionable status we like to attribute to them. Toleration would be advisable as long as it makes good political sense, but could be rejected in the name of more serious concerns, or even just popular concerns. As a matter of practice, this may already happen. That is, we may choose to ignore the rights of some people when a serious concern arises, as, for example, is often done in times of war. But when such a suspension happens, it is often seen as either a great injustice, or as an unfortunate but necessary measure given the extenuating circumstances. Even in the latter case, in most people's minds, the suspension of the right does not cast doubt on the sanctity of the right. That is, political life may sometimes require that we reorder our priorities and principles to meet a crisis, but this does not mean that our commitment to our principles is any less fervent. But if what I have argued above is correct, and if we reject God and Nature as grounds for morality,[17] in order to be consistent, we would have to be

---

[17] Like Locke, most intellectuals reject Nature as a possible ground for morality when they reject a teleological universe. But whereas Locke embraced God

willing to say that though the right is a principle that guides our political decisions, it has no real grounding or robust authority. If an
alternative political principle arose which garnered more popular support or made more sense politically, then there would be no justifiable
reason to be indignant about the suspension of such rights. This
would make incoherent indignation about the suspension of free
speech, the suspension of rights to marriage and reproduction, even
the suspension of religious freedoms and the right to believe in no
God at all. Thus, to put a fine point on the argument, a universal,
rational, secular argument would be incapable of furnishing a defense
for the universal, rational secularism we currently so wish to defend.
Perhaps, then, there is room for the pragmatist to develop more tolerance, if not respect, for the believer's position, as I think Locke's
works recommend.

---

as the only possible alternative ground, as noted above, in American intellectual
life, God has become an increasingly problematic ground.

5

RECONCILING NATURAL RIGHTS AND THE MORAL SENSE IN FRANCIS HUTCHESON'S REPUBLICANISM

Michelle A. Schwarze and James R. Zink

In this chapter, we seek to explain how important facets of Francis Hutcheson's epistemology reveal him to be far more individualistic than usually argued and illustrate how commitments to both a benevolent moral sense and a natural rights political order might be reconciled. Francis Hutcheson's thought represents one of the first efforts in modernity to understand the salutary role of the passions in moral and political life. Hutcheson aimed to explain how the passions make individuals sociable in a liberal political system, and he is well known for his claim that one passion in particular—universal benevolence—is the source of moral motivation.[1] Hutcheson described an innate "moral sense" that finds our benevolent, other-regarding actions intrinsically valuable, rendering society with other individuals both natural and pleasurable for us. In developing this moral sense philosophy, Hutcheson sought to emphasize the natural propensities distinct from self-love individuals possess in order to reveal them to be far less egoistic than he claims some of his predecessors, like Hobbes and Mandeville, characterize them to be (e.g., *Compendiaria* II.iv.I.140, III.iv.IV.283-284; *System* III.IX.iv).[2]

---

[1] John D. Bishop, "Moral Motivation and the Development of Francis Hutcheson's Philosophy," *Journal of the History of Ideas*, 57(1996): 277-278.

[2] Throughout this paper, we provide the relevant part or book, section, subsection and paragraph number for each citation from Hutcheson's works, along with the corresponding page number from the Liberty Fund translations of the *Philosophiae Moralis Institutio Compendiaria, with a Short Introduction to Moral Philosophy* (Indianapolis: Liberty Fund, 2007) [hereafter *Compendiaria*]; *A System*

However, what is perhaps most interesting about Hutcheson's thought—and most relevant for our contemporary political discourse—is that his altruistic moral claims exist alongside a strict commitment to a natural rights political philosophy. Indeed, his commitment to universal benevolence appears to be tempered by his arguments for a liberal political system which establishes protections for the individual rights of its citizens. Despite his beatific moral claims, Hutcheson argues in a noticeably Lockean way that political legitimacy is derived from a social contract entered into by individuals seeking the stable protection of their inviolable natural rights.[3] In other words, Hutcheson appears to advance a moral theory centered on an understanding of the individual as naturally embedded in a social whole and concerned with the common good, while developing a political theory firmly committed to individuals *qua* individuals and to their interests as rights-bearers. Understanding how Hutcheson resolves the tension between commitments to altruism in his moral thought and individualism as the basis for political society can therefore also help shed light on how we might encourage the development of pro-social behavior without politically mandating it.

This paradoxical relationship between Hutcheson's moral and political thought has often been overlooked in previous scholarship due to either a mischaracterization of his ethics or of his debts to other natural rights political philosophers. Specifically, efforts to distance Hutcheson from some of his predecessors, including Locke, and to emphasize his proto-utilitarianism, have led commentators to resolve this tension too quickly or without taking seriously his republicanism.

---

of Moral Philosophy (Indianapolis: Liberty Fund, 2014) [hereafter *System*]; *An Inquiry into the Original of Our Ideas of Beauty and Virtue* (Indianapolis: Liberty Fund, 2008) [hereafter *Inquiry*]; and the *Essay on the Nature and Conduct of the Passions and Affections, with Illustrations on the Moral Sense* (Indianapolis: Liberty Fund, 2014) [hereafter *Essay and Illustrations*].

[3] For a good overview of the similarities between Locke and Hutcheson on natural rights, see Samuel Fleischacker, "The Impact on America: Scottish Philosophy and the American Founding," in *The Cambridge Companion to the Scottish Enlightenment*, ed. Alexander Broadie (New York: Cambridge University Press, 2003) 316-337.

Garry Wills, for example, in a controversial book on the ideological origins of Jefferson's thought, insists that Hutcheson, not Locke, is his true intellectual progenitor.[4] Wills does this by characterizing Hutcheson's notion of right—and Jefferson's as well—as a right over others for the *common* rather than individual good, which is readily approved of by a moral sense which naturally directs us toward benevolence.[5] As Fleischacker has noted, this enterprise fails to "recognize the extent to which Hutcheson was himself indebted to Locke's political philosophy."[6] While Hutcheson posits that individuals pursue general benevolence due to their inherent moral sense, he simultaneously claims that this pursuit is not inconsistent with the protection of natural rights, because of their mutual tendency toward the greater good. This emphasis on the greater good is often what leads commentators to classify Hutcheson as a proto-utilitarian.[7] He famously concludes "that action is best which procures the greatest happiness for the greatest numbers" (*Inquiry* II.III.viii), but he tempers this consequentialist claim with a firm belief in God's beatitude as it is revealed by each *individual's* moral sense. An undue emphasis on his utilitarian leanings has thus led some to wrongly discount the seriousness of Hutcheson's commitment to natural rights. We will argue that Hutcheson instead strikes a middle ground by endorsing the pursuit of a type of innocent self-love, consistent with the pursuit

---

[4] Garry Wills, *Inventing America: Jefferson's Declaration of Independence* (New York: Mariner Books, 1978). Wills unconvincingly attempts to connect passages from the Declaration with distinct selections from Hutcheson's works, while asserting that nearly identical passages from Locke's *Two Treatises of Government* and the document itself are coincidental. Additionally, see Richard C. Sinopoli, *The Foundations of American Citizenship: Liberalism, the Constitution and Civic Virtue* (New York: Oxford University Press, 1992) in which Sinopoli aligns Hutcheson with the Anti-Federalists because of their mutual concern for fostering a "sentiment of allegiance" to the government.

[5] Wills, *Inventing America*, 215-217.

[6] Fleischacker, "The Impact on America," 321.

[7] Raphael, for example, calls Hutcheson "explicitly utilitarian," as well as the first philosopher to advocate a utilitarian ethic on empiricist grounds, see D.D. Raphael, "Hume and Adam Smith on Justice and Utility," *Proceedings of the Aristotelian Society*, 73(1972-1973): 88-9.

of benevolence, and through the protection of a myriad of individual natural rights within civil government.

In addition to sometimes unduly widening the gap between Hutcheson and Locke or overemphasizing his utilitarianism, past scholarship has not fully accounted for the effects of Hutcheson's skepticism or account of limited benevolence on his political theory. While commentators like Haakonssen remark on his skepticism about human judgment or understanding,[8] they do not trace the implications of this skepticism on his political theory generally nor specifically to his embrace of a natural rights political regime. What is more, scholars often miss some of Hutcheson's more striking claims about the limits of benevolence itself. Hutcheson is doubtful of the existence of "inflexible" goodness or benevolence (*Compendiaria* II.I.ii.112)—and his skepticism deepens when individuals in positions of authority are considered.

This chapter proceeds in three broad strokes. First, we expound Hutcheson's moral philosophy, paying particular attention to his account of the moral sense and its distinction from the common sense advocated by later thinkers in the Scottish Enlightenment, to innocent self-love and its relation to benevolence, and to human happiness and the convergence of the individual and social good. Second, we reveal the extent of Hutcheson's skepticism about both human knowledge and goodness and, subsequently, why this skepticism leads him to ardently defend individual rights both philosophically and politically. Finally, we conclude by tracing Hutcheson's influence on early American political thought, focusing on how this reconciliation of natural right and the moral sense provided some Founding-era thinkers with the intellectual resources to cultivate civic virtue within a liberal political framework. Although our concluding thoughts are only suggestive on this point, we argue it is important to connect Hutcheson's unique contribution to the political vision being developed in America without overstating it.

---

[8] Knud Haakonssen, *Natural Law and Moral Philosophy: From Grotius to the Scottish Enlightenment* (New York: Cambridge University Press, 1996) 78.

Hutcheson's Moral Thought

In this section, we unpack Hutcheson's understanding of the moral sense and self-love and explain how these concepts color his moral prescriptions and will affect the principles from which he derives his political theory. As we have mentioned, one problem with previous scholarship on Hutcheson's moral philosophy centers on a disregard for its coherence with, if not endorsement of, a certain type of individualism. Commentators like Wills present Hutcheson's work as largely irreconcilable with Locke's, a palliative to the individualistic, right-centric politics that we find in the *Second Treatise*. Yet this view of Hutcheson's purpose runs counter to Hutcheson's own understanding of his philosophical project. As Howe observes, "[t]he Scots always honored Locke and considered themselves to be working within his tradition."[9] Indeed, we show below that Hutcheson embraced natural rights, the central pillar of Lockean political philosophy, though his account of natural rights differs from Locke's in important respects.[10]

---

[9] Daniel Walker Howe, "Why the Scottish Enlightenment Was Useful to the Framers of the American Constitution," *Comparative Studies in Society and History*, 31(1989): 579.

[10] See Fleischacker, "The Impact on America," 322; Ronald Hamowy, "Jefferson and the Scottish Enlightenment: A Critique of Garry Wills's *Inventing America*," *The William and Mary Quarterly*, 36(1979): 508-509; Thomas Pangle, *The Spirit of Modern Republicanism: The Moral Vision of the American Founders and the Philosophy of Locke* (Chicago: University of Chicago Press, 1988) 37-38. To say that Hutcheson followed Locke is not to say that other influences do not appear in his writings. Some scholars classify Hutcheson as a natural law thinker of sorts who inherited his arguments for natural rights from other natural law theorists like Grotius and Pufendorf; see, for example, M.M. Goldsmith, "Regulating Anew the Moral and Political Sentiments of Mankind: Bernard Mandeville and the Scottish Enlightenment," *Journal of the History of Ideas*, 49(1988) 593; Knud Haakonssen, *Natural Law and Moral Philosophy*, 65; Carole Robbins, "'When It Is That Colonies May Turn Independent': An Analysis of the Environment and Politics of Francis Hutcheson (1694-1746)," *The William and Mary Quarterly*, 11(1954): 250.

Toward this end, we seek to explain why, as Fleischacker suggests,[11] relying upon Hutcheson as the Scot to soften the jagged individualistic edges of a rights-based politics like the one advanced by early American theorists is understandable, if ultimately some commentators extend Hutcheson's adherence to universal benevolence beyond what the author himself would have intended. As we shall see, Hutcheson argued that humans possess a natural moral faculty that complements self-love insofar as it recommends benevolence and other-regarding behavior. For someone like Wills, Hutcheson's portrait of naturally sociable and moral humans becomes the prism through which we should read Jefferson's Declaration of Independence in order to observe the Founding Fathers' kinder, gentler vision of America. Yet, while his moral theory is commonly characterized as optimistic about the prospect of individual moral improvement,[12] Hutcheson never denies the power that self-love has over human behavior, nor does he always condemn its pursuit. He consistently qualifies his claims about the reliability of universal benevolence, and an epistemological skepticism renders him even more doubtful about our critical ability to discern the intentions of others, an important consideration that inclines us either more or less toward moral action. When we consider these qualifications in light of Hutcheson's acceptance of rights-based politics, moreover, we see the potential for many of the pitfalls associated with Locke's political theory in his philosophy as well. But Hutcheson's moral philosophy extends beyond Locke's in its attempt to recast natural law theory and to incorporate

---

[11] Our analysis echoes Fleischacker's claims about Hutcheson's Lockeanism and the compatibility of the moral sense and natural right, but, unlike Fleischacker's, highlights how Hutcheson's conception of innocent self-love contributes to the particular theory of human happiness he advances, while also more concretely connecting Hutcheson's moral thought to his jurisprudence by evaluating the particular effects of his epistemic skepticism. See Fleischacker, "The Impact on America," 318-323.

[12] See, for example, James N. Loughran, "Francis Hutcheson: Benevolence as Moral Motivation," *History of Philosophy Quarterly*, 3(1986): 296-297; and Sinopoli, *The Foundations of American Citizenship*, 6.

Christian teachings into a beatific moral framework.[13] For Hutcheson, this moral sense, or *"conscience* by which we discern what is graceful, becoming, beautiful and honourable in the affections of the soul, in our conduct of life, our words and actions" (*Compendiaria* I.I.X), allows individuals to be motivated and made happy by virtuous action while simultaneously rendering the social passions naturally agreeable to them. The moral sense, then, is in fact what makes rights-based politics possible on Hutcheson's account: in principle, it counters our self-interested impulses by strengthening our inclination toward a universal, disinterested benevolence (*Essay and Illustrations* I.II.31-32), which, though naturally pleasing, is often a much weaker impetus for action.

Hutcheson on the Moral Sense, Self-Love, and Human Happiness

In response to both the natural law tradition and the egoism of Hobbes and Mandeville, Hutcheson structured his moral theory on a "moral sense" that affectively attaches individuals to one another through a naturally approved benevolence. For Hutcheson, our moral sense provides immediate perceptions of the moral qualities of actions and behavior in the same way that our external senses allow us to perceive taste, sound or images. It is a sense natural to all individuals "by which we perceive *Virtue*, or *Vice* in our selves, or others" and which is "found in some degree in all men" (*Essay and Illustrations* I.I.5-6). Hutcheson does not mean to suggest that "men have extra noses for moral smells,"[14] but rather that our ability to perceive the moral value of actions is inherent and necessary for moral reasoning.

From this inherent moral sense, Hutcheson claims that corresponding desires for the good ends suggested to us by our various senses, as well as the means necessary to achieve them, develop and direct our behavior. This includes a counter-intuitive *"disinterested"*

---

[13] Haakonssen, *Natural Law and Moral Philosophy*, 78.

[14] Elmer Sprague, "Francis Hutcheson and the Moral Sense," *The Journal of Philosophy*, 51(1954): 796.

desire for the happiness of others, or benevolence, "which we account virtuous [though] it is not *directly* excited by the prospects of any *secular Advantage, Wealth, Power, Pleasure of the external Senses, Reward from the Deity or future Pleasures of Self-Approbation*" (*Essay and Illustrations* I.I.III). Hutcheson appeals to "*universal Experience and History*" as evidence that the "*moral Senses* of Men are generally *uniform*" (*Essay and Illustrations* II.IV.282; see also *Essay and Illustrations* II.IV.285). He also emphasizes that actions or passions given approbation are perceived and judged pre-reflectively by the moral sense in the "Heat of Action" (*Essay and Illustrations* I.III.vii.86). Put differently, the moral sense naturally motivates all human beings to pursue benevolent actions because they appear immediately agreeable and not due to an immediate *interest* in assisting others. Hutcheson thus brilliantly reframes Mandeville's contention that "we are befooled into a publick Interest against our Will" (*Essay and Illustrations* I.I.iv.24) by insisting that our befuddlement stems from the natural approbation which attends benevolent public actions rather than the unintended consequences of the pursuit of our own interest. This distinction between the direct and indirect influence of self-interest and the independence of benevolence in morality is paramount for Hutcheson, as his moral education is grounded on strengthening our natural disinterested social passions.

Anticipating objections about the existence of disinterested passions and the often-indistinguishable nature of actions motivated by benevolence and those by self-interest, Hutcheson provides an example of a strong passion he believes provides no direct benefit to its possessor. The desire for "future Fame," which even "an *Epicurean* who denies a future State or one to whom God revealed that he should be annihilated" feels, is illustrative of the fact that we can often be motivated by considerations other than our own interest (*Essay and Illustrations* I.I.ii.3.24-25). Despite our inability to enjoy the advantage gained from them during our lifetimes, we still perform certain actions that would bring us no other benefit. Disinterested passions—or those passions in which self-interest has only an indirect influence—establish a natural sociability according to Hutcheson and prevent us from being solely selfish beings. As a result, he argues for a moral education grounded in the expansion of our disinterested passions and the alignment of the "Prospect of any *Interest*" and virtuous offices, so that "Rewards particularly may over-ballance all Motives to Vice" (*Essay and Illustrations* I.I.ii.3.26).

Although our moral sense recommends disinterested benevolence to us, Hutcheson makes clear that self-love can gain approbation as well. Indeed, he seeks to distinguish his theory from those "*rash* views of human Affairs" that "often represent *private Interest* as opposite to the *Publick*" (*Essay and Illustrations* II.IV.282). Hutcheson claims that representing these interests as contrary and zero-sum perverts their natural accordance. When untutored by these false philosophies, self-interest and the public interest naturally converge, making the "most necessary Point in Morals" to both engage "these Motives of *Self-Interest*" as well as "to engage Men to publickly useful Actions" (*Essay and Illustrations* II.IV.282). According to Hutcheson, an "*innocent Self-Love*" (*Essay and Illustrations* I.IV.iv.109) is morally salutary because it often encourages individuals to perform actions whose benefit redounds to the public as well as themselves. We only seem to be naturally compelled toward benevolent actions *if* they do not come in conflict with our ability to meet stronger desires, like self-interest. Hutcheson posits that, "there is in Mankind such a *Disposition* naturally, that they desire the Happiness of any known *Sensitive Nature,* when it is not inconsistent with something more strongly desired" (*Essay and Illustrations* II.VI.ii.308-309). In his treatise on aesthetics, he makes this claim even stronger: "General benevolence alone is not a motive strong enough to industry, to bear labour and toil, and many other difficulties which we are averse to from self-love...Self-love is really as necessary to the good of the whole as benevolence" (*Inquiry* II.VII.viii.284).

Contrary to the claim made by some scholars that Hutcheson excludes self-interest from virtuous action,[15] then, we see that Hut-

---

[15] Some notable examples here are Clarence DeWitt Thorpe, "Addison and Hutcheson on the Imagination," *ELH*, 2(1935): 215; Luigi Turco, "Sympathy

cheson defends "self-interest rightly understood" as a possible, though not *sole* or primary, motive for virtue.[16] By allowing self-interested actions to indirectly lead to virtue and abstaining from condemning self-love outright, Hutcheson provides a nuanced account of moral motivation rather than a myopic one. As we will show, Hutcheson's commitment to this innocent self-interest is made still more evident in his development of a political theory grounded in natural rights, which legitimizes and even lauds those self-interested pursuits that are not harmful to others.

The interest of the individual is also a focus of Hutcheson's account of the good and good offices. After incorporating a role for self-interest into his moral psychology, Hutcheson develops a theory of obligation centered on benevolence and a theory of both the individual and social good achieved through its exercise. "Supreme happiness" for the individual consists in the exercise of the nobler virtues, such as benevolence and the worship of God,[17] because the moral sense renders these actions so naturally pleasurable (*Compendiaria* I.II.xi). Yet the happiness of the individual is directly related to the happiness and good of society: the "*greatest* or *most perfect Good* is that whole Series, or Scheme of Events, which contains a greater Aggregate of Happiness in the whole, or more universal absolute Good, than any other possible Scheme" (*Essay and Illustrations* I.II.iii.37). It

---

and the Moral Sense: 1725-1740," *British Journal for the History of Philosophy*, 7(1999): 81.

[16] For an explanation of the term more broadly, see Harvey Mansfield, "Self-Interest Rightly Understood," *Political Theory*, 23(1995): 58; Some scholars who understand Hutcheson's notion of self-interest in this way include M.M. Goldsmith, "Regulating Anew the Moral and Political Sentiments of Mankind," 600, and Andrew Skinner, "Pufendorf, Hutcheson and Adam Smith: Some Principles of Political Economy," *Scottish Journal of Political Economy*, 42(1995): 166-167.

[17] Despite his insistence on a moral duty to worship God, Hutcheson makes explicit in the *Compendiaria* that freedom of religion and toleration are paramount. As he puts it, the "*right of private judgment*, {or of judging for himself in all matters of duty,} especially as to religion" is paramount because "tis plain no man can without guilt counteract his own conscience; nor can there be any virtue in dissimulation or hypocrisy" (*Compendiaria* II.IV.iii).

therefore follows that the "happiness of the whole"—which Hutcheson equates with the "universal Good" (*Essay and Illustrations* I.II.iii.34)—is produced as an *effect* of each individual's pursuit of her own happiness. When Hutcheson states that the best "course of life" for each individual is "a constant study to promote the most universal happiness in our power, by doing all of the good offices we have opportunity which interfere with no more extensive interest of the system" (*Compendiaria* I.II.xi.11), we see that we do so by pursuing our *own* happiness. Of course, Hutcheson claims that a significant proportion of our own happiness is generated through benevolent actions that further the interests of others, but it is important to note that our desire to promote universal happiness is indeed best achieved through the pursuit of individual good.

Hutcheson's Skeptical Epistemology

This commitment to individual judgment and the individual's pursuit of happiness might seem odd given the social attachment the moral sense breeds, but Hutcheson tempers his moral theory with an epistemological skepticism. Given that he claims the pursuit of benevolence is naturally recommended to all individuals, we might expect Hutcheson to suggest that a greater happiness could be attained in the aggregate if individuals more actively sought to make *others* as well as themselves happy. Yet "our *Understanding* and *Power* are limited," according to Hutcheson, such that "we cannot know many other Natures, nor is our utmost *Power* capable of promoting the Happiness of many" (*Essay and Illustrations* II.VI.ii.309). Hutcheson admits elsewhere that, as far as morality is concerned, "what seems to be most truly wanting in our Nature is greater *Knowledge, Attention* and *Consideration*" (*Essay and Illustrations* I.VI.vii.204). Faced with insurmountable difficulties in perceiving the interests of others and finite resources and capabilities, Hutcheson suggests that individuals pursue their own interests and those of others linked to them by "Ties of *Blood*" or who have revealed their intentions and interests by acting virtuously themselves (*Essay and Illustrations* II.VI.ii.309). This is not to say that Hutcheson believes we should attempt to suppress a natural desire for benevolence or the other public affections that are "not very far from a *Counter-Ballance* to the *Medium* of the Selfish" (*Essay and Illustrations* I.VI.vii.203). As we described above, Hutcheson holds benevolence generally to be the foundation of virtuous behavior and even lauds its exercise towards individuals who have previously harmed us; as he explains in a discussion on the public passions, "*Forgiving of Injuries*, and much more *returning Good for Evil*, appears wonderfully great and beautiful to our moral Sense" (*Essay and Illustrations* I.III.vi.83). Rather, Hutcheson recommends that our efforts to do positive good for others should be moderated by the degree of certainty with which we can discern their intentions and interests. Our moral sense should therefore be "regulated" (*Essay and Illustrations* I.VI.v.193) or enlightened by our reasoning on the probable outcomes of our actions and on human behavior more generally.

It is also important to distinguish Hutcheson's moral sense philosophy from "common sense" philosophy, later championed by Thomas Reid, although the two philosophies are not necessarily incompatible. In Hutcheson's thought, moral and common sense refer to two distinct processes of human understanding that occur sequentially. First, our moral sense, along with the other external senses and our "sense of honor" (*Essay and Illustrations* I.I.i.5-6), allows us to perceive moral or other qualities in various objects and relations. Subsequently, by a type of common sense or a "*little Reflection*" (*Essay and Illustrations* Preface.iv), we process the sensory information received. While Hutcheson never uses the term Reid will to describe it, his treatment of our limited understanding echoes Reid's discussion of common sense. Hutcheson claims we make use of probabilistic reasoning bolstered by common experience to understand the world in the absence of geometric certainty: "There seems to be this Degree of Liberty about the Understanding, that tho the *highest Certainty* or *Demonstration* does necessarily engage our Assent, yet we can suspend any *absolute Conclusion* from *probable* Arguments, until we examine whether this [*33*] apparent *Probability* be not opposite to *Demonstration,* or *superior Probability* on the other side" (*Essay and Illustrations*

I.II.ii.33). What is more, this inferior type of reasoning is all that is required for moral judgment. As Hutcheson states in the Preface to the *Essay and Illustrations,* a *"little Reflection* will discover the truth [about the practical principles of morality]" (*Essay and Illustrations* Preface.iv).

Hutcheson initially refers to this distinction between common sense and moral sense to separate his moral sense theory from Locke's epistemology, which he claims some have mistakenly assumed to imply that moral ideas are "independent upon a Moral Sense" (*Essay and Illustrations* II.II.252), but his claims against the incompatibility of Locke's empiricism and the moral sense can be extended to common sense philosophy as well. According to Hutcheson, both Locke's experiential account and epistemological theories centered on innate ideas cannot account for the conception of "fitness" in either the relations of inanimate objects to rational beings or between rational beings; rather it presupposes a moral sense to explain "why 'tis an *ultimate End*, not fit for any thing farther, but *absolutely fit*" (*Essay and Illustrations* II.II.253-255). Alternatively, common sense philosophers like Reid sought to defend common knowledge about and belief in the external world against the attack of both innate ideas philosophers and empiricists like Locke who, "pitying the credulity of the vulgar, resolve[d] to have no faith but what is founded upon reason."[18] They held our fallible yet reliable "common sense" to be sufficient for reasoning about and understanding our experiences.[19] However, common sense philosophy does not necessarily preclude, any more than innatism does, a moral sense that allows us to naturally perceive moral qualities. For Hutcheson, the moral sense is required for individuals to understand ultimate ends—as it allows them to perceive good and bad, respectively—as neither infinite reflection on innate ideas or those received from our other senses nor common reasoning could ever suggest when or why to prefer one equally pleasurable action to

---

[18] G.A. Johnston, *Selections from the Scottish Philosophy of Common Sense* (Chicago: The Open Court Publishing Company, 1915) 35.
[19] Johnston, *Selections from the Scottish Philosophy of Common Sense,* 28.

another. Contrary to scholars who position Reid's common sense and Hutcheson's moral sense at odds with one another,[20] we therefore argue that the two are, at minimum, consistent. It is thus unsurprising that Reid claims to agree with those philosophers who posit a moral sense and to defend a "moral sense or conscience" not unlike the one described by "Dr. Hutcheson."[21]

Natural Rights and the Limits of Human Understanding

So far, we have shown that Hutcheson's emphasis on the moral sense and the social passions that it recommends does not imply a morality of self-denial, but it is nonetheless surprising that he commits himself to an individualistic, natural rights brand of politics. Indeed, some scholars claim that Hutcheson's natural rights theory is truly "paradoxical" because he strives to defend a type of civic virtue driven by benevolence even while protecting natural rights that seem to be derived solely from self-love.[22] Why does Hutcheson defend an account

---

[20] Sinopoli, *The Foundations of American Citizenship*, 56.

[21] Reid, Thomas, *Inquiry and Essays*, ed. Ronald E. Beanblossom and Keith Lehrer (Indianapolis: Hackett Publishing, 1983) 319-320. In what seems to be a reversal of his previous position on the topic, Reid states that he "cannot help being of a contrary opinion" than the moral sense philosophers in his essay, "On Judgment," because some argue that the moral sense or taste "might have been so constituted as to have given determinations different or contrary to those they now give" (*Inquiry and Essays* 288). Yet Hutcheson, as was illustrated above, is no moral relativist. As the Hutchesonian moral sense *always* approves of the same actions and passions, like benevolence, Reid cannot have Hutcheson in mind in this critique. As Haakonssen puts it, "moral perception [for Hutcheson] is *not* a subjective affective experience; and moral judgments are thus not simply the expressions of such experiences," in Haakonssen, "Natural Law and Moral Realism," 74.

[22] James Moore, "Natural Rights in the Scottish Enlightenment," in *The Cambridge History of Eighteenth-Century Political Thought*, ed. Mark Goldie and Robert Wokler (New York: Cambridge University Press, 2006) 300; see, also, James Moore "The Two Systems of Francis Hutcheson: On the Origins of the Scottish Enlightenment," in *Studies in the Philosophy of the Scottish Enlightenment*, ed. M.A. Steward (New York: Oxford University Press, 1990); Toshiaki Ogose, "Morality, Polity, Economy in Francis Hutcheson," in *The Rise of Political Econ-*

of civil government committed to the protection of individual rights rather than the enforcement of social duties? How can his claims about the primacy of benevolence in moral life be reconciled with the minimal perfect duties defended in his political works?

We suggest that these positions seem less contradictory when viewed through the lens of Hutcheson's general skepticism. First, as outlined above, it is too easy to overemphasize the role of benevolence in Hutcheson's ethics at the expense of the nuanced defense of innocent self-love that Hutcheson provides. Second, as we explain in what follows, Hutcheson assumes a tone of general skepticism throughout his moral and political theory that carefully qualifies his claims. That is, we believe that Hutcheson's moral and political thought can be reconciled when considered in light of his skepticism about human judgment[23] and when we recognize that this skepticism characterizes Hutcheson's claims about goodness as well. On our view, Hutcheson's natural rights project was more than simply an "illuminating illustration of the difficulties of bringing natural rights and civic virtue within the confines of a single system."[24] It was the product of a genuine republican commitment that does not contradict his moral sense philosophy, even if it suggests some practical challenges.

That Hutcheson's political thought is firmly grounded in natural rights is clear, despite (or perhaps because of) his beatific moral theory and concern with the common good. Individual natural rights for Hutcheson derive from and are naturally approved by the moral sense along with the duties of benevolence described in his ethical thought. As a result of their natural approbation by the moral sense, natural rights in fact enjoy the same moral and juridical status as benevolence

---

omy in the Scottish Enlightenment, ed. Tatsuya Sakamoto and Hideo Tanaka (New York: Routledge, 2003) 41; Richard B. Sher, "Professors of Virtue: The Social History of the Edinburgh Moral Philosophy Chair in the Eighteenth Century," in *Studies in the Philosophy of the Scottish Enlightenment*, ed. M.A. Steward (New York: Oxford University Press, 1990) 96.

[23] Haakonssen provides a good overview of Hutcheson's epistemology in *Natural Law and Moral Philosophy*, especially 82.

[24] Moore, "Natural Rights in the Scottish Enlightenment," 302.

on Hutcheson's account. As he asserts when describing the origin and end of government, "the design of the civil power is both to promote peace and happiness" for citizens, as well as "an undisturbed enjoyment of all their rights" (*System* II.III.v).

But what exactly are the content of the rights Hutcheson insists are paramount protections for individuals in civil society? Essentially, Hutcheson outlines private "unalienable" (*Compendiaria* II.II.iv.124; III.III.i.273) natural rights for individuals that are the result of both "natural principles or appetites in men" and "right reason,"[25] such as a right to life or a right to private judgment (*Compendiaria* II.IV.ii.141; II.IV.ii.142), that have the highest juridical status. He grounds these rights in his account of the state of nature—one characterized by "peace and good-will, of innocence and benevolence," yet still an "infirm, uncertain condition of mankind" (*Compendiaria* II.IV.i.140)—in a manner "reminiscent of Locke."[26] This similarity with Locke continues in Hutcheson's ascription of equality to human beings in this natural state because of their role as rights-bearers. As Hutcheson says, "in this respect all men are originally *equal,* that these natural rights equally belong to all, at least as soon as they come to the mature use of reason" (*Compendiaria* II.IV.iv.143). In other words, natural rights are fundamental in Hutcheson's political thought, as they are naturally recommended to us and as they provide the basis for a natural equality that will influence his recommendations for a legitimate constitution of the civil state.

The natural approbation of individual rights is predicated on Hutcheson's description of "innocent self-love" as well. As self-love is not rejected as a possible indirect motive to virtue because the happiness of the individual redounds to the happiness of the whole, natural

---

[25] It is important to note that Hutcheson argues for natural rights on account of their derivation from *both* reason and our moral sense rather than our sentiments alone, as some scholars have claimed (e.g., Fleischacker, "The Impact on America," 321).

[26] Andrew Skinner, "Pufendorf, Hutcheson and Adam Smith: Some Principles of Political Economy," 167. See, also, Fleischacker, "The Impact on America," 320-322.

rights are approved of because they promote both individual happiness and the greater good. As Fleischacker puts it, Hutcheson "affirms the importance of rights" as Locke does, but "he provides a new basis for them."[27] Hutcheson asserts that natural rights are "pointed out by [each individual's] senses and natural appetites, recommending and pursuing such things as tend to their happiness: and our moral faculty {or conscience} and the kind motions of the soul shews us that each one should be allowed full liberty to procure what may be for his own innocent advantage or pleasure, nay that we should maintain and defend it to him" (*Compendiaria* II.IV.ii.141). The natural approbation of individual rights Hutcheson discusses in fact renders them paramount for his political prescriptions.

For Hutcheson, civil government is formed in order to render these natural rights more secure, and it is made legitimate when established and maintained in accordance with their dictates. Rights are fundamental in the creation of the state because they are fundamental to our happiness. Hutchesonian perfect rights are those whose "violation would make human Life intolerable" or "miserable" (*Inquiry* II.VII.vi.277). Thus, these natural "unalienable rights are essential Limitations in all Governments" (*Inquiry* II.VI.x.295). If a civil power has "no foundation in right," then Hutcheson claims it has an "essential defect" (*Compendiaria* III.IV.iv.283; see also *Compendiaria* III.V.i.285)—governments must be founded on *contract* in order to be just.[28] In order to legitimately form a civil government then, Hutcheson recommends a three-stage social contract, which unite all subjects together through mutual contract, determine the type of government, and obligate the subjects and sovereign to one another through a second contract (*Compendiaria* III.V.ii.286). This social contract insti-

---

[27] Fleischacker, "The Impact on America," 321.

[28] Hutcheson is so concerned with the legitimate foundation of government on individual right and consent that he insists any social contract based on the "rash deed of an ignorant people" is unbinding (*Compendiaria* III.IV.iv.283 [pg.238], II.IX.v.183 [pg. 159]). Fleischacker mentions Hutcheson's concerns with political legitimacy, but does not expand on why the protection of individual rights is requisite for this legitimacy, "The Impact on America," 321.

tutionalizes protection for both the natural rights to liberty and private judgment that Hutcheson enumerates (*Compendiaria* II.IV.iii.142).

By focusing on the protection of individual rights, we do not mean to suggest that Hutcheson is unconcerned with the good of the society as a whole when he proposes his plan for civil government. Indeed, Hutcheson makes explicit that the "end of all civil polity" is the "common interest of the whole body" (*Compendiaria* III.IV.iv.283). In identifying the end of civil government as the procurement of the common good, some scholars claim that Hutcheson weakens natural rights protections. That is, they claim that Hutcheson concludes "with great clarity that, as the moral ground for rights is the natural law about the maximization of happiness, all individual rights (including perfect rights) are defeasible by actions of greater general utility than their protection in particular cases and types of cases."[29] Hutcheson does claim a "Privilege of flagrant Necessity" (*Inquiry* II.VII.x.298) based on the "universal interest of all" that supersedes individual rights protections, but the circumstances necessary to invoke this right are so extraordinary that its legitimate exercise is exceedingly rare (*Compendiaria* II.XVI.ii).

What is more, Hutcheson's commitment to natural rights needs to be understood in light of his claims about the convergence of the individual and social good. We can see this crucial relationship between his notion of natural rights and the end of civil society when he elaborates on the second precept of "social life": natural law prescribes that we "contribute toward the general interest of society," but this contribution can be made by treating those familiar to us well or by pursuing our own innocent self-love, as "he who innocently profits a Part, contributes also in fact to the good of the whole" (*Compendiaria* II.II.iv.124). The compatibility of innocent self-love and the common good is evidenced yet again when Hutcheson claims that "No Person, or State can be happy, where they do not think their important

---

[29] Knud Haakonssen, "Hugo Grotius and the History of Political Thought," *Political Theory*, 13(1985): 258.

Rights are secur'd from the Cruelty, Avarice, Ambition, or Caprice of their Governours" (*Inquiry* II.VII.x.299). As a result of this convergence of individual and social happiness, the end of Hutchesonian government should be seen as both the protection of individual natural rights and the common good.

Hutcheson's account of the relationship between individual rights and the common good reveals how the interest of individuals and of the whole are the *raisons d'être* of civil government, but it does not indicate why Hutcheson defends a limited, natural rights political order as the best *means* to achieve those interests. To understand how his moral and political theories converge, we must carefully consider his arguments about the limits of human understanding and the flexibility of human goodness. For Hutcheson, our susceptibility to error—in both analytic and moral reasoning—gives rise to a limited government and the reservation of rights to individuals deemed most suited to discern their own interests.

Hutcheson's doubts about human understanding pervade his political theory as they do his moral theory, leading him to promote limited government and to avoid mandating positive moral duties to others. Throughout his works, Hutcheson emphasizes the "fallibility of moral judgment"[30] and the human propensity to err when considering what actions are in our best interest or in the interest of others. When Hutcheson describes the need for civil government, he assumes that even "honest men" would doubt the intentions of others to judge fairly in conflicts over the allocation of goods in the state of nature, due to our inability to assess others' intentions with certainty (*Compendiaria* III.IV.i.280). Hutcheson also highlights the "infirm uncertain condition" of our external happiness in order to explain why it is much more difficult to make another person happy than to interfere with her plans in a harmful way (*Compendiaria* II.IV.i.140-1)—a knowledge problem that leads him to defend the negative rights or

---

[30] Knud Haakonssen, "Natural Law and Moral Realism: The Scottish Synthesis," in *Studies in the Philosophy of the Scottish Enlightenment*, ed. M.A. Steward (New York: Oxford University Press, 1990) 76.

justice we have delineated. In other words, our obligation of benevolence is mitigated by our limited ability to understand other individuals and their interests. Hutcheson's skepticism about human reasoning thus proceeds from his beliefs about the difficulty involved in discerning both the intentions *and* desires of others.

Along with this limited skepticism, Hutcheson expresses reservations about human goodness, concerns that emerge even more urgently when he speaks of politicians and other individuals in positions of authority. As with his moral theory, these reservations temper Hutcheson's political proposals. In a striking statement about the uncertainty of individual goodness and the corrupting nature of political power, Hutcheson asserts that,

> since no man can give sufficient evidence to the satisfaction of all, that he is possessed even of superiour wisdom, and much less of his stable inflexible goodness; since ambitious dissimulation would always make the greatest shew of goodness, if this were a sure step to ascend to power; nor can men search into each others hearts to detect such hypocrisy: and since no power generally suspected and dreaded can make a people, who are diffident of their most important interests, easy or happy; no man can justly assume to himself power over others upon any persuasion of his own superior wisdom or goodness, unless the body of the people are also persuaded of it, or consent to be subjected to such power, upon some reasonable security given them, that the power intrusted shall not be abused to their destruction. (*Compendiaria* II.I.ii.112)

Hutcheson's deep suspicions about the individual capacity for goodness, as well as the deleterious effects of ambition for individuals in positions of power, might seem somewhat unexpected given his strong assertions elsewhere about the universality of benevolence. Yet these reservations about goodness derive from Hutcheson's doubts about human understanding. If we are unable to reliably access the intentions or desires of others, there is at least some uncertainty about whether and to what extent their intentions depart from those dictated by morality. Entrusting any individual with significant, unrestrained power—especially given the natural strength of self-love (e.g., *Inquiry* II.II.xi.161)—is an invitation for its abuse, and our "fear of mischiefs to arise either from the weakness or vices of men" is justified because not all men are "faithful" in acting according to duty (*Compendiaria* III.IV.i.279). Hutcheson's skepticism regarding both human goodness and understanding therefore lead him to propose a system of institutional constraints and natural rights protections while still advocating imperfect duties of benevolence.

Hutcheson in America

While much has been written about Hutcheson's influence in America, there is not broad consensus on the exact *nature* of that influence, something that we think is attributable in part to the apparent contradiction between his moral and political prescriptions. In his well-known essay, David Fate Norton argues that Hutcheson had a direct impact on both the revolutionary politics and political theory of the early American republic through his student and professor at the College of Philadelphia, Francis Alison, and various preachers and activists in Pennsylvania.[31] He provides evidence that Pennsylvania preachers and "humanitarians" adopted Hutcheson's innovative arguments against slavery and for a strong right to resistance and revolution, both of which were grounded in natural rights, during the revolutionary era. Indeed, he goes so far as to call Hutcheson a "champion of human rights."[32] Other scholars have joined Norton in highlighting the direct impact of Hutcheson's notion of the right to governmental resistance on the American founders[33] as well as the influence of the Hutchesonian moral sense, and the common sense philosophy espoused by Scottish philosophers like Thomas Reid, on John Witherspoon, another professor of moral philosophy at the Col-

---

[31] David Fate Norton, "Francis Hutcheson in America," *Studies on Voltaire and the Eighteenth Century,* 154(1976): 1547-68. See, also, Douglas Sloan, *The Scottish Enlightenment and the American College Ideal* (New York: Teachers College Press, 1971) 88.

[32] Ibid., 1556.

[33] See Fleischacker, "The Impact on America," 321, and, especially, Robbins, "When It Is That Colonies May Turn Independent'."

lege of New Jersey (now Princeton) and signatory to the Declaration of Independence.[34] And, as we have already seen, Wills famously attempted to derive Jefferson's ideas in the Declaration from Hutcheson's moral sense thought, using Hutcheson to significantly reinterpret that document as a call to duty and self-sacrifice. Sinopoli somewhat echoes Wills's views when he identifies Hutcheson's "altruistic psychology" with the Anti-Federalists' emphasis on smaller communities that do not extend beyond the range of individuals' benevolent sentiments.[35] As explained above, we think that some of this disagreement stems from (a) misreading his moral philosophy as one that conceives of self-love and self-interest as utterly inconsistent with our natural duty of benevolence, and (b) a failure to properly appreciate the complementary relationship between his moral theory and his natural rights political commitments.

Conclusions

Reconciling the tension between Hutcheson's moral and political theory not only helps us more precisely identify his intellectual legacy but also elucidates how a natural rights political philosophy can indeed incorporate the sentiments into civil society in a socially salutary manner. As we have argued, previous work has misunderstood both the tension between the two aspects of Hutcheson's thought and the way in which this tension can be resolved. As a result of insufficient attention to Hutcheson's support of innocent self-love, his aggregate

---

[34] Gideon Mailer, "Anglo-Scottish Union and John Witherspoon's American Revolution," *The William and Mary Quarterly*, 67(2010): 718-19, and Sloan, *The Scottish Enlightenment and the American College Ideal*, 122-25. Mailer is keen to point out that Witherspoon diverges from Hutcheson on his classification of "mercy" as an imperfect right and thus one not to be enforced by law. Yet Hutcheson does not classify "mercy" as a perfect natural right either; indeed, as we have shown, Hutcheson delineates perfect, private rights those individual rights which consist in the abstention from harm and protection of freedom of thought and conscience rather than any positive duties of benevolence.

[35] See Wills's *Inventing America*, and Sinopoli's *The Foundations of American Citizenship*, esp. pages 60-3.

theory of happiness and his skepticism about both human under-standing and goodness, some scholars have exaggerated Hutcheson's commitment to universal benevolence. This de-emphasis of Hutcheson's individualistic claims has often led commentators to discount his indebtedness and similarity to Locke and to discount the strength of the natural rights protections he advocates. To remedy this, we have expounded Hutcheson's nuanced moral sense theory, his claims about moral motivation and, finally, his insistence on the convergence of individual and social happiness within societies established firmly on political rights.

As we suggested in the final section of this paper, the manner in which Hutcheson grapples with the conflict between the individual and common good and the solutions he proposes indeed have rele-vance for our understanding of Founding-era political debates and, more generally, the intellectual heritage of American political thought and institutions.

At the time of the contentious publication of Wills's abovemen-tioned study of Jefferson and the Declaration, scholarship explaining the revolutionary and founding eras mostly broke into two camps: those who argued that the colonists—or at least the prominent statesmen among them—were animated by republican principles[36] and those who insisted that they instead operated under the influence of John Locke's natural rights understanding of politics.[37] In one

---

[36] Some notable examples include Bernard Bailyn, *The Ideological Origins of the American Revolution* (Cambridge: Belknap Press of Harvard University Press, [1967] 1992); Lance Banning, *The Jeffersonian Persuasion: Evolution of a Party Ideology* (Ithaca: Cornell University Press, 1978); Drew R. McCoy, *The Elusive Republic: Political Economy in Jeffersonian America* (Chapel Hill: The University of North Carolina Press, 1980); Gordon S. Wood, *The Creation of the American Republic, 1776-1787* (Chapel Hill: The University of North Carolina Press, [1969] 1998).

[37] See, for example, Thomas Pangle, *The Spirit of Modern Republicanism*; and Michael P. Zuckert, *The Natural Rights Republic: Studies in the Foundation of American Political Thought* (Notre Dame: Notre Dame Press, 1996). Of course, there are other possible influences, and while most scholars writing on the Amer-ican founding era tend to identify one of these influences as more powerful than

sense, Wills's general argument was not novel: as we have demonstrated, prior to *Inventing America*, other researchers had unearthed Hutcheson's influence in America[38] and, more generally, examined the impact of Scottish Enlightenment thought on important figures involved in early American politics.[39] While Wills's communitarian reading of Hutcheson, in other words, mistakenly places the Scot much farther afield of Locke than he actually was, and farther than the Americans understood him to be, it undoubtedly had the desirable effect of rekindling interest in the links between Scottish Enlightenment thinkers and the American understanding of politics. Critics

---

the other, they generally are careful to acknowledge some cross-pollination and recognize how circumstances and multiple intellectual traditions combined to shape the complex character of the era's politics. Sometimes the tone of these debates obscures the fact that these scholars agree on much. Zuckert, for example, suggests as much: "I think the affirmation of liberal modernity need not imply the simple rejection of the other options. Like several other recent writers on the founding, I have my reservations about the terms of the debate. What are taken to be exclusive alternatives often are not.... [A]lthough liberal modernity at bottom derives from a different impulse than classical antiquity or Christianity, and indeed opposes some aspects and versions of both, it yet proved able to make peace with and indeed assimilate important aspects of both." See David F. Ericson, *The Shaping of American Liberalism: The Debates over Ratification, Nullification, and Slavery* (Chicago: University of Chicago Press, 1993) for a compelling synthesis of the competing viewpoints.

[38] Some of the first arguments for the influence of the Scots in the early Republic are found in a special issue of *The William and Mary Quarterly* in 1954 dedicated to the topic, including Robbins's claim that Hutcheson's right to resistance was especially relevant for early American thinkers in "When It Is That Colonies May Turn Independent.'" Norton, "Francis Hutcheson in America," and Sloan, *The Scottish Enlightenment and the American College Ideal*, are two other important examples.

[39] For a survey, see the first section of the introduction to Richard B. Sher and Jeffrey R. Smitten, *Scotland and America in the Age of Enlightenment* (Edinburgh: Edinburgh University Press, 1990) and Fleischacker, "The Impact on America." See, also, R. G. Frey, "Moral Sense Theory and the Appeal to Natural Rights in the American Founding," in *Liberty and the American Experience in the Eighteenth Century*, ed. David Womersely (Indianapolis: Liberty Fund, 2006); Howe, "Why the Scottish Enlightenment Was Useful to the Framers of the American Constitution."

quickly descended on Wills's work and persuasively rebutted Wills's attempts to deny Locke's influence on Jefferson,[40] and some of them have gone farther to note that even if Hutcheson inspired Jefferson and shaped his political thought (which is not implausible), such an influence would not be at all inconsistent with a Lockean view of politics. Yet one question posed by Wills' study—namely, how did the Founders believe a rights-centric society could foster good citizenship and duties towards others?—received renewed interest in its wake, and a new generation of scholars redoubled the effort to understand the different ways in which Scottish philosophy shaped America's founding era political thought.[41]

---

[40] For a thorough critique of Wills's use of Locke, see Hamowy, "Jefferson and the Scottish Enlightenment."

[41] This renewed interest, in large part, was directed toward early research on the connection by intellectual historians like Clive and Bailyn and Robbins in a special issue of the *William and Mary Quarterly* devoted to the subject in 1954, and to a well-known article by Adair, among others; See John Clive and Bernard Bailyn, "England's Cultural Provinces: Scotland and America," *William and Mary Quarterly* 11(1954): 200-13; Robbins, "When It Is That Colonies May Turn Independent'"; and Douglas Adair, "'That Politics May Be Reduced to a Science': David Hume, James Madison and the Tenth *Federalist*," *Huntington Library Quarterly* 20(1957): 343-60. Again, for an overview of the development of the historical treatment of this cross-Atlantic connection, see Fleischacker, "The Impact on America," Richard B. Sher and Jeffrey R. Smitten, *Scotland and America in the Age of the Enlightenment* (Edinburgh University Press, 1990) and Richard C. Sinopoli, *The Foundations of American Citizenship*.

PART III

ON ALEXIS DE TOCQUEVILLE'S REPUBLICANISM

6

TOCQUEVILLE'S NEW SCIENCE OF POLITICS

Lise van Boxel

In his masterful work, *Democracy in America,* Alexis de Tocqueville argues a new political science is necessary to direct the inescapable democratic revolution that is overtaking the world (Introduction, 7).[1] This new science ought to direct the development of these democracies to make them as salutary as possible for their citizens. More specifically, it must establish and sustain the co-existence of equality and freedom so that the human being does not descend into a sub-human condition. According to Tocqueville, such mindful tending will yield a basically decent, if rather uninspiring, human being. The highest, most brilliant peaks of human potential will be lost, but so too will the most dreadful forms of oppression and enslavement. Tocqueville's analysis of modern democracy remains amongst the most thoughtful and thorough. It behooves us, therefore, to study the goals he sets for the new science thoroughly. Yet, we may also wonder whether the new science he conceives points beyond the limits he envisions for it. I will outline some particular tasks Tocqueville sets for his new political science before suggesting how it might become more fully what it is.

Tocqueville introduces his new science by noting the way in which it is original. He observes that heads of state have never before thought of preparing for an inevitable change to the form of their

---

[1] Alexis de Tocqueville, *Democracy in America*, translated by Harvey Mansfield and Delba Winthrop (Chicago: The University of Chicago Press, 2000). All subsequent references to this work will either refer to the section title and page number or will include the relevant volume number, part number, chapter number, and the page or range of pages.

regime (Introduction, 7). They have faced such change without fore-sight, or they have fought uselessly against it. Including himself amongst these statesmen, Tocqueville says it is as if "we" have been "placed in the middle of a rapid river" with our eyes fixed obstinately "on some debris that we still perceive on the bank, while the current carries us away and takes us backward toward the abyss" (Introduction, 7). Thus, the development of the democratic revolution has so far been left to luck and accident. The new science aims to replace accident with mind.

With this as his goal, Tocqueville offers his vision of the best form of modern democracy, and thus the form at which the new science should aim. In his own words, "men will be perfectly free be-cause they will all be entirely equal; and they will all be perfectly equal because they will be entirely free" (2.2.1, 479). In the context of this salutary marriage between equality and freedom, Tocqueville speaks of both conditions in limited, political terms. Equality denotes equali-ty under the law: everyone is subject to the same laws and no one is above them. Such equality does not imply equality of wealth or any other extra-legal conditions. It is therefore properly contrasted with the legally sanctioned inequality that characterizes aristocratic re-gimes. Aristocracies have laws, but they are not the same for every-one. Rather, one is legally subject to different laws according to what place one occupies in the political hierarchy. The meaning of free-dom, as it is used in this context with equality, is similarly limited and political. It signifies the legally sanctioned right to participate in gov-ernment. So defined, it stands in contradistinction to slavery, the condition in which one is legally forbidden from such participation.

Implicit in Tocqueville's vision of an ideal democracy is the claim that freedom and equality are not equivalent and indeed are separable. This fact is vividly apparent in an appeal and warning Tocqueville gives to his fellow aristocrats, whom he thinks are facing the inevitable loss of their regime. Since they do not have the option of maintaining the status quo, they have only two choices, both of which must be new. They can either extend the political freedom they have to the people, or they can reduce all the people to slavery:

If men had to arrive, in effect, at the point where it would be necessary to make them all free or all slaves, all equal in rights or all deprived of rights; if those who govern societies were reduced to this alternative of gradually raising the crowd up to themselves or of letting all citizens fall below the level of humanity, would this not be enough to overcome many doubts, to reassure consciences well, and to prepare each to make great sacrifices readily? (1.2.9, 301)

Initially, one might think freedom is the main issue that is at stake in these options. Upon further reflection, however, we see it is equality, not freedom, that is of primary interest. Freedom already exists in an aristocracy, albeit in varying degrees according to the political hierarchy. The condition of equality, by contrast, is new, and it characterizes both of the options Tocqueville presents. In both, everyone is equal under the law. The difference consists in whether they are all equally regarded as citizens who enjoy the same legal rights, or whether they are universally levelled to what Tocqueville calls a sub-human condition. In this condition, everyone is equal in legal insignificance. The rulers alone are politically free, but they are no longer rightly defined as aristocrats. The general condition of sub-humanity together with the fact that the rulers stand above the law mean these rulers are despots.

The options Tocqueville outlines reveal equality is not at odds with a political condition of sub-humanity, but political freedom is. One cannot be both free and in a sub-human state. It is therefore freedom, not equality, that keeps one from falling below a condition that is proper to a human being. This conclusion lends itself to the additional, democratic inference that, since all human beings are equal as humans, all ought to be politically free. This reasoning constitutes the fundamental premise of the ideal form of democracy Tocqueville envisions. So understood, equality justifies freedom, and vice versa.

In what way is freedom proper to the human condition? The implicit association Tocqueville makes between these two things invokes the Western tradition in political philosophy and, in particular, its most famous founders: Socrates, as depicted by Plato, and Aristotle. According to these philosophers, natural beings have a final end or state of completion that is given to them by nature. Such completion for the human being consists in the philosophic life. In its fullness, this life includes sufficient knowledge of the good, and of the good for the human being in particular, to enable the philosopher to lead a good life, for he rules himself according to his knowledge. Thus, we may reasonably say there is both an intellectual and moral component to the philosopher and to his way of life, where morality signifies the desire and ability to act in accordance with the good. This self-rule is the fullest form of freedom. It is not only beneficial and pleasant, according to these philosophers, but also good in itself.

Neither these ancient philosophers nor Tocqueville thinks most people are able to become philosophers. However, Tocqueville does seem to think all human beings can be basically decent. Indeed, he endorses the idea, articulated by another thinker, that the freedom for all citizens to do just and good things is a beautiful expression of the kind of freedom democracy can afford (1.1.2, 42-3). Both this notion of freedom and the philosophic freedom previously described extend beyond the limited definition of political freedom Tocqueville employs when he speaks of the salutary marriage between equality and freedom. Nevertheless, the expansive concept of freedom serves as a high-minded goal toward which Tocqueville looks, and he thinks democratic people and statesmen would be well served by aiming at it as they work to secure and uphold political freedom.

Since freedom, even in its limited, political form, is what keeps human beings above a sub-human condition, whereas equality lends itself "almost as readily" to despotism as to democracy, we might like to think it is freedom that is especially characteristic of this form of regime (1.1.3, 52). This assumption would be wrong. In his effort to determine whether equality or freedom constitute the essence of democracy, Tocqueville reasons that freedom exists in every government, for the ruler is always politically free. Since political freedom is a universal attribute of government, it cannot be the defining characteristic of any one form of regime (2.2.1, 481). By process of elimination alone, therefore, we can conclude equality must be the essence of democracy. This conclusion accords with the first observation Tocqueville offers regarding democracy in America, and the one with which he introduces his book:

> Among the new objects that attracted my attention during my stay in the United States, none struck my eye more vividly than the equality of conditions. I discovered without difficulty the enormous influence that this primary fact exerts on the course of society; it gives a certain direction to the public spirit, a certain turn to the laws, new maxims to those who govern, and particular habits to the governed.
>
> Soon I recognized that this same fact extends its influence well beyond political mores and laws, and that it gains no less dominion over civil society than over government: it creates opinions, gives birth to sentiments, suggests usages, and modifies everything it does not produce. (Introduction, 3)

Although Tocqueville limits the concept of equality in his formulation of the best democratic regime to political equality, his opening remarks clearly indicate political equality has repercussions that extend far beyond equality under the law. Equality permeates democracy in America. What is true of America in this regard is true of democracy per se, according to Tocqueville. In America, he notes, democracy exists in a more advanced form than in any of the other emerging democratic nations. They are all moving toward what America is. It is therefore equality, not freedom, that characterizes the worldwide democratic revolution. In light of this discovery, we can reformulate the immediate task of the new political science: it must guide the development of equality so that it is married to freedom.

Tocqueville goes on to note that democratic people's attachment to equality is ardently passionate. This might seem benign enough, until we consider it in conjunction with the fact that equality can readily accommodate despotism. Considered together, these conclusions indicate democratic people will always prefer equality; thus, at least when pressed, they will resign their freedom in favor of enslavement rather than tolerate privilege. Tocqueville makes this point chillingly:

> [F]reedom is not the principal and continuous object of . . . [demo-
> cratic people's] desire; what they love with an eternal love is equali-
> ty; they dash toward freedom with a rapid impulse and sudden ef-
> fort, and if they miss the goal they resign themselves; but nothing
> can satisfy them without equality, and they would sooner consent to
> perish than to lose it. (1.3.5, 53; see also 1.3.5, 52-3; 2.2.1, 481)

One can give a reasoned account of why a political condition that combines equality and freedom is preferable to other forms of regimes. Tocqueville makes several such arguments. Absent this combination, is the democratic people's vehement attachment to equality defensible? According to Tocqueville, it is not. As the options he sketches for the aristocrats reveal, freedom is good in itself, whereas equality is neither good nor bad. It may become good or bad depending on whether it is allied with freedom.

The fact that Tocqueville thinks the attachment to equality alone is indefensible does not mean he thinks it cannot be understood, but only that it cannot be rationally defended. Indeed, he offers multiple explanations for this non-rational phenomenon. They can be summarized as follows: unlike freedom, equality is easy to sustain; its benefits are obvious; and it is ours. Regarding the relative ease of sustaining equality, Tocqueville observes it requires almost no attention: "the pleasures of equality offer themselves" (2.2.1, 481). Acquiring and maintaining freedom, by contrast, involve sacrifice and ongoing attention, for "to lose political freedom, it is enough not to hold it, and it escapes" (2.1.1, 480). Tocqueville goes on to note that the perils of what one might characterize as excessive freedom—namely, anarchy—are more obvious than those that attend excessive equality. Unfortunately, the blatant perils of excessive freedom are not counterbalanced by the overtness of the goods it affords. On the contrary, "[t]he goods that freedom brings show themselves only in the long term, and it is always easy to fail to recognize the cause that gives birth to them," whereas "the advantages of equality always make themselves felt from now on, and each day one sees them flow from their source" (2.2.1, 481). The final reason for democratic people's preference for equality—that is, an ignorant attachment to what is our own simply because it is ours and hence without regard to its true goodness—is, philosophically, the least respectable reason. Tocqueville describes it as follows:

> Do not ask what unique charm men in democratic ages find in liv-
> ing as equals, or the particular reasons that they can have for being
> so obstinately attached to equality rather than to the other goods
> that society presents to them; equality forms the distinctive charac-
> teristic of the period they live in; that alone is enough to explain
> why they prefer it to all the rest. (2.2.1, 480)

While this attachment may be exasperating from a rational per-spective, the inclination to love one's own without adequate judgment of its genuine value is so pervasive and embedded in human beings that this explanation is not only the deepest of the accounts, but it also describes the most dangerous threat to the salutary marriage of equality and freedom.

An exploration of this ignorant love sits at the heart of "Book One" of Plato's *Republic*, which in turn lays out the theme of the work as a whole. In "Book One," we find Socrates conversing with a group of politically ambitious youths about the meaning and intrinsic worth of justice. Polemarchus, who is the most philosophically promising of the interlocutors, suggests justice consists in helping friends and harming enemies. Socrates responds by asking him whether he con-siders his friends good because they are his or whether they are his friends because they are good.[2] He thereby implicitly points out that those who believe their friends are good simply because they are their own lack judgment and are instead motivated by an unexamined pas-sion. In other words, they are controlled by prejudice, which includes but is not limited to an ignorant form of self-love. If they are guided by prejudice regarding such personally significant and urgent matters

---

[2] Plato, *The Republic of Plato*, translated by Allan Bloom (United States: Basic Books, 1991) 332c - 335e.

LISE VAN BOXEL

as love and friendship, then it is very likely they also lack judgment when faced with any other issue (see 2.1.1, 406; 1.2.7, 244). In sum, therefore, these human beings are un-free in terms of the highest meaning of freedom.

Polemarchus understands the distinction Socrates makes and the point of his question. His capacity to recognize his ignorance, together with his interest in overcoming it, indicate he is philosophically promising. Are democratic people able to recognize that their attachment to equality is based in ignorance? Can we expect them to feel a significant urge to overcome this ignorance and to replace it with knowledge? If their attachment could be informed by knowledge, the problem that is of such concern to Tocqueville would be resolved. Knowledge would lead them to subordinate their attachment to equality to the good, which is allied with freedom. Hence, to the extent that they remained attached to equality, they would demand that it always be accompanied by freedom.

Tocqueville does not think a full philosophic education is a viable solution for a democratic populace. He does not fault democratic people in particular for their lack of philosophic promise. Rather, he expects every multitude to be dogmatically attached to the opinions that most characterize it, and he does not expect any multitude to overcome these prejudices by becoming philosophic (e.g. 1.2.3, 179; 1.1.2, 43-4; 1.2.5, 188-9). Philosophers are always exceptional, whereas a multitude, by definition, never is.

While it may be futile to try to educate a democratic population to subordinate its passion for equality to its knowledge of the good, one can guide and manipulate the passion itself so that it is more aligned with a love of the good and hence with a love of freedom. This is precisely the route Tocqueville takes. He discerns that the attachment to equality is, in fact, the effect of two very different passions. He characterizes one of them as virile, or strong and legitimate.[3] This noble or virtuous passion has an expansive nature that

---

[3] Alexis de Tocqueville, *de la Démocratie en Amérique, I* (Paris: GF-Flammarion, 1981) 115. The full passage in the original French language is:

incites those who feel it "to want all to be strong and esteemed" (1.1.3, 52). Motivated by its desire for this goal, it tends "to elevate the small to the rank of the great" (1.1.3, 52). This passion's attachment to greatness reveals its inherent belief in, and love of, the good, which in turn makes it an ally of freedom.

The second passion that produces a vehement attachment to equality is envy—the recognition of the good accompanied by the desire to destroy it and those who possess it. Since this passion aims to destroy the good, it is an enemy of freedom. In its attachment to equality, therefore, it expresses itself as a "depraved taste . . . that brings the weak to want to draw the strong to their level and that reduces men to preferring equality in servitude to inequality in freedom" (1.1.3, 52; see also 1.2.5, 188-9; 2.1.1, 406; 2.4.3, 645).

The fact that the virtuous attachment to equality entails the effort to elevate oneself and all human beings indicates this passion is characterized by a sense of potency. One who feels it expects he will continue to secure good things for himself and others. The envious attachment to equality is, by contrast, characterized by a sense of impotence. The envious human being recognizes the good, and he wants it. However, he does not act to secure it because he does not feel powerful enough to do so. He feels hopeless. Rather than exerting himself, therefore, he seeks to destroy those who have the good. In other words, he is spiteful out of the sense of his own weakness.[4]

Given these considerations, we can infer that, if one wants to foster the virtuous attachment to equality and to destroy or marginalize the vicious attachment, one ought to make democratic people feel

---

Il y a en effet un passion mâle et légitime pour l'égalité qui excite les homes à vouloir être tous forts et estimés. Cette passion tend à élever les petits au rang des grands; mais il se rencontrre abuse dans le Coeur humain un gout deprave pour l'égalité, qui porte les faibles à vouloir attire les forts à leur niveau, et qui réduit les homes à préférer l'égalité dans la servitude à l'inégalité dans las liberté.

[4] For an illuminating discussion on envy, including its distinction from jealousy, with which it is often confused, see Aristotle, "The Rhetoric," in *The Complete Works of Aristotle: The Revised Oxford Translation,* edited by Jonathan Barnes (Princeton: Princeton University Press, 1985) 1387b 22—1388b 5.

as empowered as possible. Tocqueville draws the same conclusion. He is very clear about the connection between the sense of potency and high-mindedness on the one hand and impotence and baseness on the other (e.g. 2.2.5, 490). The problem he also sees very acutely, however, is that modern democracies, left to themselves, drastically increase their citizens' sense of impotence. As a single person in the face of vast numbers of people, and with no special political powers of his own, the democratic individual feels his political inefficacy.

This experience of political weakness is exacerbated by the democratic individual's belief that the majority is both wiser and carries more moral weight than any individual, including himself. Thus, he is inclined to conclude neither he nor anyone else has the right, as an individual, to exercise whatever little power he might have. Tocqueville notes that these potentially enervating beliefs arise from the insufficiently examined association democratic people make between the idea of political equality on the one hand, and the intellectual and moral authority of the majority on the other. Democrats believe "there is more enlightenment and wisdom in many men united than in one alone, in the number of legislators than in their choice. It is the theory of equality applied to intellects" (1.2.7, 236). He then adds: "The moral empire of the majority is also founded on the principle that the interests of the greatest number ought to be preferred to those of the few" (1.2.7, 237).[5]

As noted, this pervasive sense of impotence augments envy, which in turn threatens freedom (e.g. Introduction, 9-10; 1.2.5, 188-9; 2.1.1, 406; 2.4.3, 645). Even individuals who are not prone to envy nevertheless suffer from the sense of their inefficacy in ways that are bad for the prospects of freedom. The feeling of political impotence inclines them to withdraw from public into private life, where they

---

[5] Tocqueville is especially concerned about the belief that the interests of the many should be preferred to those of the few because it tends to support the tyranny of the majority. To counter this potentially unjust prejudice in favor of the majority, Tocqueville makes a reasoned appeal to natural right, which serves to protect the rights of individuals in the face of the majority. See 1.2.7-8, 235-64.

become increasingly isolated and politically apathetic (e.g. 2.2.8, 503). Their withdrawal, combined with the sense that the central government represents the intellectually and morally superior majority, result in an increasing centralization of government power. "This concentration of powers, at the same time that it singularly hinders the good conduct of affairs, founds the despotism of the majority" (1.1.8, 145).

All the dangers that arise from equality contribute to the centralization of government. This vastly powerful, over-arching government then threatens to become a new kind of despot, which Tocqueville argues is the greatest opponent to freedom the world has ever seen. Since "the thing is new," Tocqueville seeks "in vain an expression that exactly reproduces the idea" and "contains it" (2.4.6, 662). With what appears to be considerable distress, Tocqueville states emphatically that "the old words despotism and tyranny are not suitable" means to understanding this new despotism, for its powers extend beyond anything the old world despots could ever reasonably hope to have, and the enslavement it produces is of a different, more durable sort (2.4.6, 662). The old form involves rule by one or a few human beings. As we shall see shortly, the new form does not involve the direct rule of human beings at all. It is Kafkaesque in character.

In the absence of a definition, Tocqueville resorts to a detailed description of what we now call administrative despotism. His extended account of it is worth reading, not only because this form of despotism is still relatively unrecognized, but also because he thinks modern democracies so susceptible to it:

> I see an innumerable crowd of like and equal men who revolve on themselves without repose, procuring the small and vulgar pleasures with which they fill their souls. Each of them, withdrawn and apart, is like a stranger to the destiny of all the others: his children and his particular friends form the whole human species for him; as for dwelling with his fellow citizens, he is beside them, but he does not see them; he touches them and does not feel them; he exists only in himself and for himself alone, and if a family still remains for him, one can at least say that he no longer has a native country.

Above these an immense tutelary power is elevated, which alone takes charge of assuring their enjoyments and watching over their fate. It is absolute, detailed, regular, far seeing, and mild. It would resemble paternal power if, like that, it had for its object to prepare men for manhood; but on the contrary, it seeks only to keep them fixed irrevocably in childhood; it likes citizens to enjoy themselves provided that they think only of enjoying themselves. It willingly works for their happiness; but it wants to be the unique agent and sole arbiter of that; it provides for their security, foresees and secures their needs, facilitates their pleasures, conducts their principal affairs, directs their industry, regulates their estates, divides their inheritances; can it not take away from them entirely the trouble of thinking and the pain of living?

[I]t confines the action of the will in a smaller space and little by little steals the very use of it from each citizen. Equality has prepared men for all these things: it has disposed them to tolerate them and often even to regard them as a benefit.

Thus, after taking each individual by turns in its powerful hands and kneading him as it likes, the sovereign extends its army over society as a whole; it covers its surface with a network of small, complicated, painstaking, uniform rules through which the most original minds and the most vigorous souls cannot clear a way to surpass the crowd; it does not break wills, but it softens them, bends them, and directs them; it rarely forces one to act, but it constantly opposes itself to one's acting; it does not destroy, it prevents things from being born; it does not tyrannize, it hinders, compromises, enervates, extinguishes, dazes, and finally reduces each nation to being nothing more than a herd of timid and industrious animals of which the government is the shepherd. (2.4.6, 662-3)

Administrative despotism arises from the convergence of centralized governing power with centralized administrative power. As Tocqueville notes, America already has a centralized government (1.2.8, 251). The only way to avoid administrative despotism, therefore, is to prevent the existing centralized government from acquiring administrative power.

Administrative power will not be acquired suddenly by the central government, since, if it were, the citizens would likely resist it.

Rather, the combination of powers will result from administrative powers creeping their way into the centralized government and accumulating there. Each little creep will appear to be beneficial, and so the majority will be inclined to accept it as good. By the time this new form of despotism is fully recognizable for what it is, it will be entrenched, and we will likely have become too infantilized to resist the temptations it offers us in exchange for our freedom.

Given these considerations, Tocqueville wisely argues that the people's love of freedom, which attends the virtuous attachment to equality, must be purposefully stimulated and strengthened in order to prevent any advance toward administrative despotism. He offers advice about how to do this both directly and indirectly. I will outline an example of each approach. Both are ingenious, for in them Tocqueville finds a means of directing equality, the most serious, unavoidable, and foreseeable threat to freedom, in such a way that it actually supports the very thing it would otherwise crush.

One of the major ways Tocqueville thinks freedom can be strengthened directly is by civil associations (2.2.5, 489). He regards these associations as a kind of democratic analogue for the role fulfilled by individual aristocrats in an aristocracy. Aristocrats are sufficiently few in number and sufficiently powerful that they can exercise their political freedom effectively as individuals. In a thriving aristocracy, the aristocrats' proud sense of their freedom inspires them to protect and preserve it. In democracies, this kind of independent action is ineffective. Yet, the democratic individual can join civil associations, which do wield power in a democracy, and become proud of what he can accomplish as part of this collective movement. Thus, Tocqueville concludes that democratic individuals should amalgamate their energy and freedom into this form of collective action.

To promote associations, Tocqueville argues a statesman must do two things. First, he must make individuals more, rather than less, cognizant of their equality with their fellow citizens. Second, he must heighten the individual's awareness of his weakness as an individual. Both suggestions amount to impressing on the individual the sense of his own insignificance and impotence. Paradoxically, therefore,

Tocqueville's advice initially seems more likely to increase, rather than decrease, the possibility of despotism.

After advocating what appear to be two very dangerous steps, Tocqueville flips what seems to be a sure path to despotism on its head. He insists that, at the same time that the statesman does these two things, he must also multiply associations. With this combination of elements, Tocqueville plans simultaneously to make the individual aware of his powerlessness as an individual, while also giving him a path to power and political freedom by means of collective action.

By exercising political freedom effectively in and through a civil association, the democratic citizen's sense of his political freedom is invigorated, and he becomes more jealous of it. In addition to enlivening his sense of freedom, he acquires both the habit of acting politically in a group and the practical education that is necessary for effective action in this mode. Such habits and experiences, together with his sense of empowerment, draw him out of his isolation and move him into public and political life more generally.

The enlivening civil associations Tocqueville advocates here are local rather than national. The step from the private life of the individual to a concern for national politics, or even to a concern for state politics, is too great for the individual to take immediately. Tocqueville realizes local associations are much more likely to attract the democratic individual's interest than political action that encompasses a broader scope, because local associations address issues that are more vividly and concretely identifiable by the individual as relevant to his life. Do not try to tell him before he has been part of any civil association that he must be active in national and state politics to secure his political freedom. He will hear the words, but they will not impress him, and he will remain unmoved. The threats and the concepts are too abstract to seem real to him. He can be roused, however, by the question of whether or not a local road needs to be relocated, especially if the proposed location would cut across his property (2.2.4, 487). In such a circumstance, the connection between his private life and the public realm is strikingly apparent to him; thus, he will be very inclined to involve himself with the decision. What begins as a local and particular exercise of political freedom has a relatively direct path to political freedom at the state and national levels (2.2.4, 486-8; 1.2.8, 274).

Tocqueville augments his direct means of bolstering freedom with indirect means. Of the latter, Tocqueville presents Christianity as the most significant. Indeed, he may regard it as the most significant of all forms of support for political freedom in a democracy. His use of Christianity for this end is once again paradoxical, since Christianity places its adherents in what he calls a condition of "salutary servitude" (2.1.2, 408-9). Tocqueville justifies his acceptance of, and support for, such servitude with the observation that no human being can examine all of his opinions. "Individual independence can be more or less great, but it cannot be boundless" (2.1.2, 408-9). The degree to which one is enslaved is variable, but some degree is inevitable. Given that, one ought to ensure one's enslavement is beneficial. In a democracy, he reasons, people's enslavement to Christian dogma is salutary because it helps to compensate for the pervasive intellectual weakness that necessarily characterizes all democracies.

According to Tocqueville, such weakness is the unavoidable effect of the general intellectual leveling that accompanies the democratic love of equality. It is further exacerbated by the lack of opportunity that exists for intellectual development, which in turn follows from the fact that most people have to work to support themselves in a democracy and therefore lack sufficient leisure for intellectual development. Finally, the fact that most people must work, combined with the democratic inclination to believe that what is common is good, produce a culture in which practicality and work for work's sake are prized more highly than the leisurely or liberal exercise of the intellect—that is, intellectual activity that is not primarily utilitarian or employed to solve predetermined problems. This pervasive societal contempt for leisurely intellectual activity is a serious disincentive to democratic individuals who might otherwise be attracted to it. Finally, the lack of opportunity for leisurely learning, even for those who endeavor to pursue it, prevents the maturation of the intellect, since its highest development depends on this leisurely activity (see 1.1.3,

50-1; 1.2.5, 188-90). Thus, although Tocqueville appreciates the goodness of democracy in so far as it offers political freedom to more people than any other type of regime, he also notes with regret that democratic peoples are amongst those most enslaved to opinion and prejudice. They have neither the time nor the inclination to engage in the most rigorous and highest philosophic or scientific pursuits (see 1.1.3, 50-1; 1.2.6, 234-7; 1.2.7, 244-5).

Although the deepest and fullest form of intellectual activity "is inaccessible to most" in a democracy, the need for the conclusions such study yields remains, as it does in any regime, "indispensable to all" (2.1.5, 418). The problem to be solved, therefore, is how these conclusions can be given to a people who cannot arrive at them independently, fully, or with adequate knowledge of how they arrived at them. According to Tocqueville, Christianity offers the best solution to this dilemma. It ameliorates the absence of the most rigorous and highest science in democracies by providing its adherents with crucial general ideas. These generalities do not capture the full complexity and subtlety of the issues they address, but they do offer enough information to "furnish a solution for each of . . . [the] primordial questions that is clear, precise, intelligible to the crowd, and very lasting" (2.1.5, 418; see also 1.2.5, 188-9; 2.1.1, 406).

At least initially, the promotion of salutary servitude in the mouth of one who would preserve freedom is shocking enough, at least before we hear his defense of it. Tocqueville's use of Christianity becomes more shocking still when he argues it should aggressively appropriate to itself the most seductive characteristic of an administrative despotism—namely, the alleviation of suffering. In other words, Christianity should become a great administrative power. How will the Church's appropriation of this power not enervate rather than invigorate freedom? Did Tocqueville not warn us that great administrative powers contribute to despotism?

It will be helpful in addressing these questions to consider the characteristics Tocqueville thinks are essential to the health and longevity of any religion in a democratic age. First and foremost, he contends that such a religion cannot involve itself directly in the governing power of the regime. So long as it is supported only by "senti-ments that are the consolation of all miseries, it can attract the hearts of the human race to it" (1.2.9, 284). As soon as it becomes united directly with the governing power, it is "compelled on occasion to oppose human beings who love it" and to intermingle with "allies giv-en it by interest rather than love" (1.2.9, 284). It thereby becomes "mixed with the bitter passions of this world," and thus loses the au-thority it could otherwise enjoy (1.2.9, 284).

Second, it must be flexible enough to adapt to the rapid political change and tumult that are characteristic of democratic epochs (1.1.2, 43-4). To attain and retain this flexibility, the religion must "find its force in the sentiments, instincts, and passions that one sees repro-duced in the same manner in all periods of history" (1.2.9, 285). Thus, it defies time (1.2.9, 285). By contrast, if it entangles itself with time-bound issues and the passions that attend them, it will pass away, like all temporal things: "[W]hen a religion wishes to be sup-ported by the interests of this world, it becomes almost as fragile as all the powers on earth. Alone, it can hope for immortality; bound to ephemeral powers, it follows their fortunes" (1.2.9, 285).

Finally, a religion that is to survive in a democratic era cannot have detailed regulations about how individuals must conduct their lives. Adherence to such regulations depends on an authoritative reli-gious leader; yet, such a leader will not command authority among democrats because his claim to special individual power does not ac-cord with their love of equality (2.1.5, 419-20). The attachment to equality disinclines people from believing in or having much respect for anyone, including a religious leader, who claims to be authorita-tive and who grants himself privileges. Thus, according to Tocque-ville, "[a] religion that would become more minute, inflexible, and burdened with the small observances at the same time that men were becoming more equal would soon see itself reduced to a flock of im-passioned zealots in the midst of an incredulous multitude" (2.1.5, 421-2).

By Tocqueville's account, Christianity in America has all the traits necessary for it to thrive throughout the democratic age. He adds that it also has the advantage of being deeply rooted in American history and culture. Whether we realize it or not, Christian mores permeate private and public life in America. Indeed, Tocqueville thinks Christianity is so deeply rooted in this nation that one could not get rid of it even if one wanted to do so. Rather than fighting uselessly against its power, he advises one ought to use it to help sustain the coexistence of equality and freedom (e.g. Introduction, 10-3).

The same ahistorical quality that accounts for Christianity's durability in a democratic age also explains why Tocqueville thinks it is safe to allow Christianity to appropriate great administrative power. By placing this power in the church, Tocqueville intends to circumvent or forestall the democratic tendency to centralize all power and thus to add centralized administrative power to the centralized governing power that already exists. Thus, he simultaneously finds a bulwark against administrative despotism; acknowledges a democratic people's attraction to an administrative power that offers relief from suffering; and finds in the Christian church what he regards as the safest means of responding to this desire to alleviate suffering.

Near the end of his book, after having outlined direct and indirect ways in which the new political science can foster freedom, Tocqueville describes what is arguably the most elevated and foundational task of politics, the creation of great human beings:

> [S]overeigns in our time seek only to make great things with men. I should want them to think a little more of making great men…and to remember constantly that a nation cannot long remain strong when each man in it is individually weak, and that neither social forms nor political schemes have yet been found that can make a people energetic by composing it of pusillanimous and soft citizens. (2.4.7, 672)

This task comes as a surprise. Throughout most of the book, Tocqueville seems to be more concerned with preventing human beings from slipping below a properly human life than with elevating human beings to unusual heights. His emphasis follows at least partly from his conclusion that democracy makes greatness nearly, if not entirely, impossible. Now, very late in the game, he speaks of using political art to make great human beings. How is this possible?

While Tocqueville's use of civil associations and Christianity to preserve freedom are strategies that are compatible with each other, neither strategy seems compatible with making great men. Associations exacerbate the individual's sense of his own weakness and give him the habit of acting only in conjunction with others. By the time Tocqueville visited America, this sense and habit were already so entrenched that they prompt him to remark: "[T]here is scarcely an undertaking so small that Americans do not unite for it.... [They] seem to see in it the sole means they have of acting" (2.2.5, 490). By contrast, great men—human beings who engage in political action on a grand scale—must be capable of acting independently.

Truly great freedom must also rise above common opinion. Nothing grand can be circumscribed by the conventions that necessarily guide collective behavior. Yet, Tocqueville argues Christian doctrine in democracies is comprised primarily of common opinion, which is accepted as true without question by democratic peoples (2.1.2, 408-9). The use of Christianity as an indirect means of protecting freedom is therefore also incompatible with the creation of great human beings. How, then, are great human beings to be created?

Tocqueville says art must be employed to this end. What art does he have in mind? He says nothing of how the new political science could be used for this purpose. Rather, he seems to differentiate between the new political science and its tasks on the one hand, and the art of creating great men on the other. This separation suggests he envisions using an art other than the *new* political science to create great human beings. Indeed, he seems implicitly to suggest the *old* political science should be employed for the latter purpose: making great human beings has arguably always been the predominant concern of political philosophy. However, the old political science is incompatible with the new political science. Each depends on its own concept of the human being, and these concepts are mutually exclusive.

More specifically, whereas the new political science directs the evolution of the emerging, indeterminate democracies, the old political science is not employed to guide the evolution of its object, the human being. The old science does not do this or even aim at doing this because it presupposes a fixed human nature—a nature that is trans-cultural, ahistorical, and that imposes an upper limit on human greatness. This conception of the human being is characteristic of the classical political philosophy of Plato's Socrates and Aristotle. Guided by the presupposition that there is a fixed limit to human greatness, the role of the sovereign, as conceived by the old political science, is to use the political art to actualize this limit in those human beings who have the potential to attain it.

Although Tocqueville seems to have the old political science in mind when he speaks briefly of creating great souls, he explicitly rejects the classical conception of a fixed human nature. According to Tocqueville, the human being is distinguished from all other animals by its perfectibility (2.1.8, 427-8). Has Tocqueville adequately considered the full implications of this doctrine? Fully considered, perfectibility means there is no limit or boundary on what the human being might become; hence, there is no limit to human greatness. The human being, like the democracies being formed by the revolution, is indeterminate. Since the new political science is a science that guides the development of the indeterminate human things, it is as applicable to the evolution of the human being as it is to the future of democracy.

Nevertheless, Tocqueville does not seem to extend the purview of the new political science to the creation of human beings and of great human beings in particular. Instead, he seems to limit its application to emerging democracies. This limitation cannot hold. One cannot place a boundary upon an art of indeterminacy. The art must be as flexible and indeterminate as the objects it directs. Thus, the new political science Tocqueville envisions points beyond his use of it. It escapes Tocqueville's grasp and finds a fuller actualization of itself in guiding the evolution of the human being.

If Tocqueville had seen the full implications of the doctrine of perfectibility alongside the full implications of the science he invents, perhaps he would not face the prospects for the human being in a democratic age with such a fatalistic and occasionally melancholy tone. The possibilities for the emerging democracies and for the human being are more varied and greater than Tocqueville expects, if only because they are more than he or any of us can know with certainty. Fatalism and resignation to accident have no place in the face of such unknowns. Fear, courage, and even exhilaration are more fitting. They are more appropriate responses to a future that is blown wide open by Tocqueville's new science, and they give us a better chance of making the best of the opportunities our indeterminateness affords us.

7

TOCQUEVILLE ON MODERN INDIVIDUALISM

Christine Dunn Henderson

Individualism is one of the hallmarks of the modern era. While the citizen of the ancient republic might be viewed as subordinating self to *polis*, the citizen of the modern republic separates himself from his regime and puts himself first. This is the vision of modern individual freedom embedded in and celebrated by Benjamin Constant in his famous 1819 speech at the Athénée Royal, in which he compares the liberty of the ancients to the liberty of the moderns. For Constant, ancient liberty is a kind of collectivized liberty—the public sphere or the life of the *polis* is vast, encompassing domestic and foreign policy, but also extending into areas such as education, religious belief, and social relations. Participation in political life and subordination of the private to the public is required of the ancient citizen, who exercises his liberty through active membership in the polity. Constant observes that in the ancient world, "No importance was given to individual independence, neither in relation to opinions, nor to labour, nor, above all, to religion," adding that "the authority of the social body interposed itself and obstructed the will of the people."[1]

Modern liberty, by contrast, is found in the space between the citizen and the polity. The independence of the individual is the very core of modern liberty, and thus, representative government, the rule of law, and guarantees of rights and of civil liberties are modern liberty's signifiers, for they indicate the presence of a robust private sphere, in which individuals exercise their liberty by choosing their own ways of life, and pursuing their own ends. John Stuart Mill's *On Liberty* (1859) is perhaps even more clear than Constant in articulating a

---

[1] Benjamin Constant, *Political Writings*, ed. Biancamaria Fontana (Cambridge: Cambridge University Press, 1988) 311.

modern vision of liberty that privileges the individual and endorses individualism. *On Liberty* begins by asserting that in all things that concern the individual, "his independence is, of right, absolute. Over himself, over his own body and mind, the individual is sovereign."[2]

If both Constant and Mill are partisans of modern liberty's individualism, between them stands Alexis de Tocqueville, who was a keen though critical student of the former and a major influence upon the latter, and who assesses modern individualism quite differently. Far from simply endorsing the individualism we moderns tend to celebrate, Tocqueville is deeply ambivalent about it, acknowledging individualism's positive potential while also warning of its dangers. Tocqueville's analysis of individualism is suggestive of a deeper ambivalence he has about modernity in general, or about life under the ever-extending equality of conditions.

This chapter looks more closely at Tocqueville's analysis of modern individualism. It begins by exploring what he means by "individualism," turning next to individualism's possibilities, and then considering individualism's dangers to both the individual and society. Finally, it examines some of the remedies Tocqueville sees to the problem of individualism, endeavoring to situate those remedies within a broader context of Tocqueville's thought and analytic method.

Tocqueville, who was responsible for the transmission of the relatively new French word *"individualisme"* into English to describe a social state characterized by atomization and isolation,[3] believed he was describing a modern phenomenon resulting from the breakdown of older, aristocratic orders and the inevitable spread of equality of

---

[2] J.S. Mill, *On Liberty and other writings*, ed. Stefan Collini (Cambridge: Cambridge University Press, 1989) 13.

[3] See James T. Schleifer, *The Making of Tocqueville's "Democracy in America"* (1980; reprint, Indianapolis: Liberty Fund, Inc., 2000) 305-6. Although Koenraad W. Swart locates the first English usage in the 1839 translation of Michel Chevalier's *Society, Politics, and Manners in the United States*, Henry Reed's translation of the 1840 *Démocratie en Amérique* certainly was responsible for the term's popular diffusion. (See Koenraad W. Swart, "Individualism in the Mid-Nineteenth Century, 1826-1860," *Journal of the History of Ideas*, 23:1 [Jan.—March, 1962]: 86.)

conditions. The aristocratic life that was slowly being displaced by equality's spread was one characterized by both immobility and connectedness. Within the aristocratic order, each person occupied a fixed place in his/her social class and thus in the socio-political universe. Aristocracies linked people together horizontally, as members of the same social class, and also vertically, with people in all positions along the social hierarchy connected to each other in a chain of reciprocal duties and obligations, running both up and down the hierarchical ladder. In aristocracies, writes Tocqueville, "each citizen always sees above him a man whose protection he needs, and below he finds another whose help he can claim."[4]

The class rigidity characteristic of aristocratic society also strengthened temporal links, so that individuals understood themselves as parts of generational chains, connected to their progenitors as well as to their descendants. The general effect of such a connected perspective is that identity is defined less in terms of the specific individual, and more in terms of the larger whole or community, whether that community be hierarchical [i.e., intra-class], feudal, or temporal. Within aristocratic societies, then, individuals "are almost always tied in a close way to something that is located outside of themselves, and they are often disposed to forget themselves" (2.2.2, 883).[5]

With the fading away of aristocracy, however, the links among individuals also weaken or disappear. Rather than seeing themselves as parts of a larger, connected line or group, democratic individuals view themselves as essentially alone, or alone except for the small circle of friends and family immediately surrounding them. As natural Cartesians, they also believe their own judgment is sufficient; within the context of individualism's emergence, their Cartesianism trans-

---

[4] Alexis de Tocqueville, *Democracy in America*, ed. by Eduardo Nolla and transl. by James T. Schleifer (Indianapolis: Liberty Fund, Inc., 2010) 883. All subsequent references to *Democracy in America* will be made within the main text, with page numbers corresponding to this edition.

[5] "Pour le meilleur et pour le pire, l'homme dans la société inégalitaire était, de fait, relié aux autres hommes." (Agnès Antoine, *L'impensé de la démocratie* [Paris: Librarie Arthème Fayard, 2003], 26.)

lates into a radical self-sufficiency, and the belief that they have no need of their fellow members of society beyond their own, chosen circle of family and friends. To borrow Tocqueville's image, if aristocracy can be represented as a great chain, linking men together in varieties of ways, democracy destroys the connections between and among classes and groups, leaving each man an isolated link, little connected beyond himself.

Although there is some similarity between egoism and individualism, Tocqueville takes pains to separate the two concepts in *Democracy in America*. Egoism is an exaggerated form of self-love and self-preference. It is rooted in the passions, and it is natural to man, in the sense that egoism is found in all eras and under all social conditions. Individualism, by contrast, is something Tocqueville understands as peculiar to democratic ages, for it is rooted in the individual's perception of himself as independent and equal to the other members of society.[6] As Pierre Manent observes, the individual "does not want to be subjected to the influence of another and does not claim to exercise such influence himself."[7] Unlike passionate egoism, individualism finds its source in the intellect, as a calculation or judgment by the individual that he is self-sufficient and that connection to the broader group of one's fellows is unnecessary. It is "a considered and peaceful sentiment"—and Tocqueville's usage of sentiment does not deny the intellectual or calculating element—"that disposes each citizen to isolate himself from the mass of his fellows and to withdraw to the side with his family and his friends; so that, after creating a small society for his own use, he abandons the large society to itself" (2.2.2, 882).

But the calculation from which individualism derives is actually a miscalculation, or what Tocqueville calls an "erroneous judgment"

---

[6] Jean-Claude Lamberti describes individualism as a sickness of an infantile or youthful democracy, whereas Daniel Jacques casts it as a sign of an unhealthy democracy. See Jean-Claude Lamberti, *La notion d'individualisme chez Tocqueville* (Paris: Presses Universitaires de France, 1970) 58; Daniel Jacques, *Tocqueville et la modernité* (Québec: Les Éditions du Boréal, 1995) 70.

[7] Pierre Manent, *Tocqueville and the Nature of Democracy*, trans by John Waggoner (Lanham, MD: Rowman & Littlefield Publishers, Inc., 1996) 54.

(2.2.2, 882). Individuals are not naturally isolated; they are born into families and communities, and as we will see, they do need their fellow citizens, both in simple and more complex ways. Moreover, if a regime based on equality is to remain free, it needs a robust public sphere, with citizens who are engaged both politically and civically.[8] To think otherwise is, in Tocqueville's view, a "failing of the mind" (2.2.2, 882), and a potentially perilous one at that.

Before turning to the dangers to which individualism might give rise, it is important to investigate the possibility that individualism might yield positive effects. Certainly, a case can be made that detaching oneself from the ties of the past and/or the ties of family, class, or clan can be good for the individual, for such detachment could allow the individual to stretch to the fullest, to become aware of possibilities that would not otherwise be discernable, to make use of his talents and abilities in pursuit of those possibilities, and to believe himself capable of attaining—through his own efforts—whatever he desires. This is the classical liberal vision of individualism familiar to us from thinkers like Constant or Mill. This vision is not absent from Tocqueville, for it is also the spirit that fuels the transformation he saw taking place in the United States: the felling of forests and the navigation of rivers, the constant motion that so struck him during his visit to America. This sense of individual empowerment lies behind the desire for self-improvement that prompts the individual to leave his home (perhaps even before he has finished building it!), and to head West, in hopes of a better life for himself and his family. Individualism's empowering side is at the heart of the great risks undertaken by American merchants, in the hopes of great profit—something so striking and unique to Tocqueville that he called it "a kind of heroism" (1.2.10, 641).

---

[8] To emphasize the civic dimension here seems consistent with Tocqueville, for although that aspect is muted in these opening discussions of individualism, it is prominent in the discussions of aristocracies that are immediately prior. There, the horizontal and vertical links between individuals are cast as links between citizens.

But while the passages in which Tocqueville describes this empowering aspect of individualism are inspiring, these examples are ultimately the exceptions, rather than the rule.[9] Just as constant agitation turns out to be enervating more frequently than it is empowering, the individualism that is celebrated by much of modernity tends, in Tocqueville's view, to have negative and dangerous results for both the individual and society. Tocqueville hints at the problems he associates with individualism with a comment he makes about democracy in his initial discussion of individualism. He says, "Not only does democracy make each man forget his ancestors, but it hides his descendants from him and separates him from his contemporaries; it constantly leads him back toward himself alone and threatens finally to enclose him within the solitude of his own heart" (2.2.2, 884). While the passage refers to democratic individualism's effects on the individual, those effects also have significant consequences on society, for they facilitate the two great dangers to which democracy is prone: tyranny of the majority and soft despotism.

In considering the effects of individualism on the individual, it is important to keep in mind that, for Tocqueville, radical independence is generally overwhelming and disempowering. This motif runs throughout the 1840 *Democracy*, figuring prominently in Tocqueville's discussions of the Americans' philosophic method (2.1.1), the need for dogmatic beliefs (2.1.2), and the need for fixity in the religious realm to counter the constant flux of the democratic political realm (2.1.5). Perhaps most strikingly, this theme is central to Tocqueville's Volume I discussions of the tyranny of the majority, in which the collective moral and intellectual weight of the Many far exceeds the individual's sense of his own importance. Standing alone against a majority, the individual is generally incapable of resisting that majority's decisions and views. Tocqueville observes, "The same equality that

---

[9] Tocqueville's placement of them in the final chapter of volume I, in which he announces his intention to consider things that are "American without being democratic" (1.2.10, 516) suggests that they are not the usual effects of individualism. Moreover, to the extent that commercial ambition fuels materialism, such ambition potentially increases dangerous individualism and threatens liberty.

makes him independent of each one of his fellow citizens in particular, delivers him isolated and defenseless to the action of the greatest number" (2.1.2, 719). In the extreme case, the majority's moral and political authority stifles all individual action and—even more ominously—all thought that run counter to its will. Tocqueville is particularly worried about the effects of majority tyranny over thought, for the end of independent thinking would be the end of freedom, and he fears that "after breaking all of the obstacles that were formerly imposed on it by classes or men, the [democratic] human mind would bind itself narrowly to the general wills of the greatest number" (2.1.2, 724). Ever alert to the soft sides of power and disempowerment, Tocqueville is also aware that the prospect of acting alone can be overwhelming, and that should fear prevent individuals from exercising their strength by acting and thinking independently, the "muscles" of liberty will atrophy from disuse. Without exercising capacities for independent thought or action, individuals will easily be absorbed into the conformity and mediocrity of the democratic "herd."[10]

If individualism eventually diminishes individuals' capacities to act and think as well as their faith in their capacities to do these things, it also constricts the range of their concerns and, ultimately, the capacities of their very souls. The individualist judges that his well-being and the well-being of a narrow circle of family and friends are the only things with which he ought to be concerned. As we have seen, however, this judgment is erroneous; the individual has failed to understand that he has duties as well as rights. He has overestimated his independence and has forgotten that he is connected to others in broader ways, as a member of a community, a city, a nation, and the human race. Indeed, some of our most noble, generous, and fully human actions and sentiments spring from a sense of our connectedness to others, beyond the semi-selfish connections of family and close friends. Tocqueville emphasizes that human hearts—and human capacities—are expanded by thoughts, feelings, and actions that look

---

[10] Marvin Zetterbaum, *Tocqueville and the Problem of Democracy* (Stanford: Stanford University Press, 1967) 76.

beyond the individual and beyond calculations of simple self-interest. By exclusively focusing on the self and its immediate concerns, individualism constricts the heart, shrinks the soul, and narrows man's possibilities for greatness, for humanity, and ultimately, for liberty.

While the contracted souls and feelings of powerlessness produced by atomizing individualism are clearly harmful to the people who experience them, they are also dangerous to a free society. All despotisms, believes Tocqueville, maintain themselves by separating their individual subjects and by ensuring that no connections form between or among people. Because democracy yields individualism which in turn yields isolation, despotism "is particularly to be feared in democratic centuries" (2.2.4, 889). But the form of despotism about which Tocqueville worries in ages of equality is a new form, one which, like individualism, is a phenomenon new to democratic ages. This soft despotism presents a gentler face than its ancient predecessors, for it "degrades" men rather than "tormenting" them overtly (2.4.6, 1248). Democratic individualists are ready material for this subtler despotism; already disconnected from their fellow citizens and absorbed in their own affairs, they are little inclined to participate in public affairs. The government plays to their self-absorption, promising to "free" them of the duties of self-government, thus relieving them of the burden of taking care of themselves and their fellow citizens, and providing them with more time and energy to pursue their own interests and pleasures.

Thus, rather than requiring citizens to turn away from their private concerns and devote themselves to public affairs or to the fatherland, soft despotism encourages a turn *away* from public-spiritedness. It makes use of selfish instincts and encourages the individual to focus on his own well-being, particularly his material well-being. Indeed, soft despotism's ideal citizen is precisely the narrow individualist, for it "calls good citizens those who withdraw narrowly into themselves" (2.2.4, 888).[11] Softly despotic government "likes the citizens to enjoy

---

[11] Tocqueville's description of the citizen of a soft despotism is eerily similar to his description of the narrow individualist: "Each one of them, withdrawn

themselves, provided they think only about enjoying themselves. It works willingly for their happiness, but it wants to be the unique agent for it and the sole arbiter; it attends to their security, provides for their needs, facilitates their pleasures, conducts their principal affairs, directs their industry, settles their estates, divides their inheritances; how can it not remove entirely from them the trouble to think and the difficulty of living?" (2.4.6, 1251).

Soft despotism is *not* a form of paternalism, for unlike a parent who hopes to prepare a child for eventual adulthood and its accompanying responsibilities, soft despotism "seeks only to fix them irrevocably in childhood." It exploits individualism's narrow self-orientation and tries to further the feelings of weakness that individualism can breed. Beginning with small matters, soft despotism deprives citizens of their choice-making capacities, leading them gradually "to relinquish the use of their will [and finally to give up on themselves]" (2.4.6, 1259). Soft despotism endeavors to shape individuals who do not value independence of mind and who, through lack of practice, become incapable of independent thought and decision-making. In an unpublished manuscript fragment, Tocqueville notes that the essence of humanity lies in the free exercise of the will.[12] By incrementally robbing individuals of their desire and ability to make free choices, democracy's new despotism robs them of the essence of their humanity, rendering them more animal-like than human. In the words of the main text, soft despotism "little by little steals from each citizen even the use of himself," until the nation is filled only with "a flock of timid and industrious animals, of which the government is the shepherd" (2.4.6, 1252).

Having seen the dangers to the individual and to society that Tocqueville believes arise from individualism, it remains to explore

---

apart, is like a stranger to the destiny of the others; his children and his particular friends form for him the entire human species; as for the remainder of his fellow citizens, he is next to them, but he does not see them; he touches them without feeling them; he exists to himself and for himself alone, and if he still has a family, you can say that at least he no longer has a country" (2.4.6, 1249-50).

[12] "All of man is in the will," notes Tocqueville (1251, n. m).

the remedies he proposes. *Democracy in America* emphasizes at least two specific remedies, free institutions (particularly local ones) and associations.[13] Not only are these remedies related, but taken together, they point to a broader plan to combat individualism, one which is consistent with the approach to solving problems seen throughout *Democracy in America* and with Tocqueville's methodology more generally.

Free institutions, which require citizen participation, combat individualism by bringing men who would otherwise be absorbed in private concerns into public affairs. This is particularly true at the local level, where power has deliberately been fragmented, so that there are more opportunities for citizen engagement in public life.[14] While American political life in general is predicated on the idea that "each person is best judge of what concerns himself alone, and the one most able to provide for his individual needs" (1.1.5, 132),[15] local political life works to refine that judgment by helping democratic individuals discover that they do need their fellow citizens, and that their personal interest is indeed connected to the interest of the whole. Tocqueville's famous remark that "Town institutions are to liberty what primary schools are to knowledge" (1.1.5, 102) nods at this dimension to participation in local political life.

---

[13] In its ability to connect individuals and to lift democratic man's gaze to something above himself and his material interests, religion is also a weapon against individualism. Yet in this sense, religion functions just like any secular voluntary association; thus, my discussion of associative life should be understood as including those aspects of religion. For a recent discussion of religion as a check to democratic individualism, see chapter 3 of Alan S. Kahan's *Tocqueville, Democracy, and Religion: Checks & Balances for Democratic Souls* (Oxford: Oxford University Press, 2015).

[14] Tocqueville's word is "scatter" (1.1.5, 112).

[15] This Constantian point is also made at 108, with a slightly different emphasis; beyond the American context, a discarded fragment emphasizes a variant on the same liberal principle, commenting that "the greatest effort of the government much tend toward teaching citizens the art of doing without its help" (900, note n).

By participating in town government, individuals are "dragged" out of their preoccupations with themselves, at least momentarily (2.2.4, 889). Being required to participate in political life teaches democratic men that they are citizens as well as private individuals, and that as citizens, they possess not merely rights but also duties. In this sense, local political life works to restore an aspect of aristocratic society lost in democratic times. Through local political involvement, democratic individualists also come to realize that their long-term private interest is often best served by tending to the public interest, and while the basic judgment about individual liberty that underpins American life remains true, political participation works to re-shape democratic man's understanding of the scope of his independence, bringing him closer to his fellow citizens and to the interest of the whole. Local political activities "constantly bring men back toward each other despite the instincts that separate them, and force them to help each other" (2.2.4, 892). To the extent that the citizen connectedness as achieved through local political participation helps democracy guard against despotism, Jean-Claude Lamberti's comment that liberty "is a product of a certain type of society....and of a certain relation between that society and the governing power" is accurate.[16]

Associative life, which Tocqueville views as the "mother science" of democratic societies (2.2.5, 902), complements local political involvement, for it plays a similar role in countering the atomization and isolation that individualism creates. By uniting with fellow citizens to solve problems or advance a cause, associative life teaches two lessons which are essential to preserving liberty in an era of democratic individualism. On the one hand, citizens discover their collective strength as they come together. This counters the feelings of powerlessness that can be produced by equality of conditions, teaching citi-

---

[16] Jean-Claude Lamberti, *Tocqueville and the Two Democracies*, transl. by Arthur Goldhammer (Cambridge, MA: Harvard University Press, 1989) 174. Whether Tocqueville follows Rousseau in believing that the fundamental political problem (in a democracy, at least) is to "denature" man and to "transform the individual into a citizen" is more contestable (Lamberti, *La Notion d'individualisme*, 12).

zens that by working collectively, they are strong enough to solve their own problems and that they therefore do not need to turn to the central powers for solutions. Standing between the individual and the central power, associations function as quasi-aristocracies, taking the place of "the powerful individuals that equality of conditions has made disappear" (2.2.5, 901).

On the other hand, associative life also moves individuals beyond themselves, connecting them to their fellow citizens and helping to reverse the contraction of horizon, spirit, and heart caused by narrow individualism. Emphasizing the expansive potential of associations, Tocqueville writes, "Sentiments and ideas are renewed, the heart grows larger and the human mind develops only by the reciprocal action of men on each other" (2.2.5, 900). Associative engagement follows the same pattern as political engagement, beginning out of self-interest, then becoming a habit, and finally, something that is enjoyable and desirable for its own sake. As Tocqueville says, "You first get involved in the general interest by necessity, and then by choice; what was calculation becomes instinct; and by working for the good of your fellow citizens, you finally acquire the habit and taste of serving them" (2.2.4, 893). Not only are the heart and spirit expanded through this process, but Tocqueville also sees associative involvement as a means by which the slide into soft despotism might be reversed.

Tocqueville's account of how engagement with others transforms interest into desire raises the question of Tocqueville's methodology in trying to solve the problems associated with modern individualism. Tocqueville has many "standard" methodologies—such as his deployment of conceptual pairs (e.g., aristocracy and democracy; America and France; etc.), his use of paradox, or his habit of beginning with the micro-observation in order to adduce a macroprinciple. One of his preferred problem-solving methods is the Madisonian tactic of solving a problem by multiplying the source of the problem. For example, Tocqueville is aware that a free press can be dangerous, but his solution is to have many newspapers, thereby diluting the strength of the danger from any single source.[17]

In thinking about the problem of individualism, one might expect that the solution would be more individualism, more turning only to oneself. Instead, Tocqueville says that Americans solve the problem of individualism—which is a problem cast as arising from equality—with liberty. The question is whether this is a departure from his usual methodology of solving a problem with more of a problem, and I want to suggest that it is not, for in trying to solve the problem of individualism, Tocqueville is really treating a problem of self-interest.

Individualism, as we have seen, is understood by Tocqueville to be caused by a "failing of the mind" (2.2.2, 882). The individualist who believes that his own good is best served by abandoning concern with the good for the whole and by withdrawing entirely into the concerns of private life has judged wrongly about the means to his chosen end—he does not understand where his true interest lies. Tocqueville's solution to the problem of individualism involves correcting the error of judgment that leads to this excessive (and excessively narrow) self-interest. Via free political and associative life, individuals come to understand that their own good is not separate from the good of the community, and that their private interest and the interest of their fellow citizens are blended. Tocqueville's solution to the defective reasoning that produces individualism is not to stop people from thinking about themselves; such a course would be folly, given human nature and a human heart in which self-interest is "the only fixed point" (1.2.6, 391). Rather, his solution to the problem of individualism is to use interest, and by tutoring the self-interested individual's judgment, to transform self-interest to self-interest well understood.

---

[17] We see this in many places in Tocqueville's thought, including his discussions of the freedoms of young girls, of the dangers associations might pose, and of political liberty more generally.

8

ALEXIS DE TOCQUEVILLE AND
ABRAHAM LINCOLN ON
MODERN REPUBLICANISM

Aristide Tessitore

Tocqueville and Lincoln were contemporaries although there is no indication that either was aware of the other.[1] Nevertheless, they held much in common on the issue of slavery and its consequences for republican government. Both were morally opposed to slavery, although neither thought there was any simple way to end it in America; and both considered its institution to be directly at odds with the political self-understanding of the American republic, which gives a central place to principles of equality and liberty.[2] Moreover, both Tocqueville and Lincoln admired the handiwork of the founding generation

---

[1] Tocqueville lived from 1805-1859; Lincoln from 1809-1865.

[2] About slavery, Lincoln writes: "I am naturally anti-slavery. If slavery is not wrong, nothing is wrong. I can not remember when I did not so think, and feel" (Letter to Albert B. Hodges, April 4, 1864). In his speech on the Kansas-Nebraska Act (1854) he explains: "I object to it [slavery] because it assumes that there can be moral right in the enslaving of one man by another. I object to it as a dangerous dalliance for a free people—a sad evidence that, feeling prosperity we forget right—that liberty, as a principle, we have ceased to revere." These citations (and all Lincoln citations) are taken from *The Writings of Abraham Lincoln*, edited by Steven B. Smith (New Haven and London: Yale University Press, 2012) pp. 418 and 66 respectively. Tocqueville's moral and political views on American slavery appear in many different passages of *Democracy in America*. See esp. 1.1.2 and 1.2.10. References to *Democracy in America* are taken from the Mansfield-Winthrop edition (Chicago and London: University of Chicago, 2000). I have also utilized Eduardo Nolla's four-volume bilingual edition with supplemental notes, translated from the French by James Schleifer (Indianapolis: Liberty Fund Press, 2010).

and the form of government established by the Constitution.[3] Although both recognized the *in*sufficiency of the principle of self-interest ingeniously deployed throughout that document as a sentinel for public safety and a guarantee of liberty, they also shared a common concern to see the form of government established by the Constitution endure.[4]

Framing the Constitution

Notwithstanding the fundamental importance of the Constitution for understanding the distinctive character of the American republic, it does not by itself provide an adequate account of the American political experience. Among other reasons, it does not articulate a deep shared purpose that might hold America together at a time of grave internal crisis. This led both Lincoln and Tocqueville to place the Constitution within a larger framework provided by other important aspects of American political history. Whereas both point to the importance of religion and warn about the dangerous tendency of Americans to ignore politics in the unfettered pursuit of material well-being, the *deepest difference* in their understanding of modern republicanism is suggested by the very different political experiences

---

[3] Tocqueville marvels at the peaceful process by which Americans gave themselves a new constitution and considered it a singular achievement, something genuinely "new in the history of societies." Regarding those who assembled in Philadelphia to produce it, he maintains that they "included the finest minds and noblest characters that had ever appeared in the New World" (1.1.8, 106-7). Lincoln's early Address to the Young Men's Lyceum (1838, *Writings*, 7-14) calls for a "political religion" characterized by reverence for the Constitution and the accomplishments of the founding generation. See also notes 18 and 19 below.

[4] Although Tocqueville is willing to endorse the Enlightenment doctrine of self-interest well understood, unenlightened self-interest is at the heart of what he considers to be the three greatest dangers threatening modern republicanism: tyranny of the majority, the problem of individualism and the drift toward soft despotism. Lincoln's great challenge was to show that America was bound together by something deeper than the conflicting self-interest of North and South, which threatened to dissolve the initial success of the American experiment in self-government.

to which each turns to supplement or contextualize America's "fundamental law" (as the Constitution is described by Hamilton in *Federalist* 78).

In Lincoln's case, he draws upon the political principles Jefferson had articulated with remarkable concision in the American Declaration of Independence. About this document, and particularly the principles articulated in its famous (and controversial) second paragraph, Lincoln maintains that they constitute "the definitions and axioms of free society" (Letter to Pierce and others, April 6, 1859). In stark contrast, Tocqueville reaches back even further to the "first age of the American republics" more than two-hundred years earlier (1.1.2, 41), where he highlights the Puritan ability to combine in a "singular and original" way "the *spirit of religion* and the *spirit of freedom*" (1.1.2, 32 and 43). According to Tocqueville, not only does this Puritan "point of departure" reveal "the character of Anglo-American civilization in its true light" (1.1.2, 43), but he writes in his now-classic book, *Democracy in America*, that it also contains "the seed of what is to follow and the key to almost the whole work" (1.1.2, 29).

Lincoln's reliance on the Enlightenment philosophy encapsulated in Jefferson's Declaration of Independence and Tocqueville's elevation of a religious-political experiment in New England that he describes as exuding "an air of antiquity and a sort of biblical perfume" (1.1.2, 33), point to two remarkably different historical events in the American experience. More deeply, they direct us to what are arguably the two most important and formative roots of American political culture: namely, the influence of Enlightenment philosophy on one hand, and that of Biblical religion on the other. This difference is made even sharper by the fact that Tocqueville barely mentions America's war for independence and is completely and surprising silent about the Declaration of Independence that provided its public justification. In sharp contrast, Lincoln traces the origin of the American republic to this period—1776 to be precise—and sees in the Declaration of Independence an expression of the core beliefs that bind the American republic together. In fact, Tocqueville explicitly subordinates the period during which Americans won their independence (1775-83) to the period and manner by which the Americans gave themselves a new Constitution (1787-89). Whereas Tocqueville describes the former as the kind of event "that every century has been able to furnish," he maintains that the latter was something genuinely "new in the history of societies" (1.1.8, 106). Tocqueville marvels at the fact that during a period of national crisis precipitated by the woefully inadequate Articles of Confederation, Americans were able to take two full years to discover without haste or fear a remedy for their failing government and then voluntarily submit to their new Constitution "without its costing humanity one tear or drop of blood" (ibid.).

If Tocqueville snubs the Declaration of Independence and demotes the importance of the revolutionary period in American history, Lincoln explicitly embraces exactly the opposite priority. He describes the Constitution as a "frame of silver" containing "an apple of gold" (Fragment on the Constitution and Union, c. January 1861).[5] The gold in question is of course the Declaration of Independence and especially its luminous second paragraph. Whereas the Constitution was the product of hard-fought and hard-won political compromises that furnished America with its "fundamental law," the famous second paragraph of the Declaration of Independence, based especially upon Lockean political philosophy, describes the principled basis for severing America's colonial ties with Great Britain.[6] In Jefferson's

---

[5] The metaphor of apples of gold framed by a picture of silver is found in Proverbs 25:11 and was used by Alexander Stephens in a letter to Lincoln on December 30, 1860. Lincoln made a note of the metaphor, using it to clarify the relationship between the Declaration and the Constitution. Since he never used the metaphor in his public speeches, it is only preserved and briefly developed in fragmentary form (*Writings*, 321-322). Although the date of the text is unknown, it was believed to have been written after reading Stephens' letter and before Lincoln's inauguration on March 4, 1861. It is generally dated "c. January 1861."

[6] Jefferson considers Locke to be one of "the three greatest men that have ever lived, without any exception" because of his contribution to "moral sciences" (Letter to John Trumbull, February 15, 1789). Michael Zuckert offers a lucid account of the distinctive character of the American experiment as a whole and the Declaration of Independence in particular as "the regime based on nature, the

final reflection on the significance of the Declaration of Independence, he viewed it as a document of world-historical significance, one that encouraged "all" peoples "to burst the chains" by which they bind themselves and "to assume the blessings and security of self-government" (Letter to Roger C. Weightman, June 24, 1826). This perspective is remarkably similar to Lincoln's own understanding of this document. About its author, Lincoln writes, "All honor to Jefferson—to the man who, in the concrete pressure of a struggle for national independence by a single people, had the coolness, forecast and capacity to introduce into a merely revolutionary document, an abstract truth, applicable to all men and all times" (Letter to Pierce and Others, April 6, 1859). What accounts for these two very different political judgments about America's public justification of its decision to assume the status of a sovereign republic?

Two Political Judgments, One Cause

Both the centrality of the Declaration of Independence to Lincoln's statesmanship as well as its glaring absence in Tocqueville's multivolume study of the American republic are traceable to one and the same cause—what Lincoln refers to as the "abstract truths" contained in the Declaration of Independence. Whereas Lincoln turned to the principles articulated in the Declaration of Independence as an authoritative expression of a pre-existing and principled unity that was at the time being eclipsed by the competing interests of North and South, Tocqueville's more historical cast of mind consistently eschewed abstract principles as a source of guidance in political matters. Indeed, he considered them to be a cause of dangerous political extremism and inept, even if at times well-meaning, political leadership. His position on this matter is given its clearest expression in *The Old Regime and the Revolution*. Rather than provide an analysis of Ameri-

---

regime ordered to natural rights," in which the influence of John Locke looms large as one of three opposing traditions contributing to the Anglo-American political tradition. See *Natural Rights and the New Republicanism* (Princeton N.J.: Princeton University Press, 1994) esp. 3-25.

can democracy based on general or universal philosophic principles, Tocqueville sought to direct the attention of his readers to the crucial political importance of "mores," specific characteristics that develop slowly over a long period of time and are unfailingly imbedded in a particular historical and political tradition.

In Tocqueville's usage "mores" do not primarily refer to a code of conduct that regulates interactions in polite society, such as exhibiting conventionally proper manners at a dinner party; rather, they refer to something far more substantial. In fact, Tocqueville explicitly indicates that he uses "mores" in its ancient or classical meaning, which refers not only to "habits of the heart," but also to the "notions," "opinions" and "ideas" by which the "habits of the *mind* are formed" (emphasis added, 1.2.9, 275). Far from describing the often helpful but at times elaborately frivolous social conventions associated with eating, grooming and courtesy, "mores" for Tocqueville describe those habitual ways of both feeling and thinking that give expression to one's deepest convictions about how one should live; that is, the opinions, notions, ideas, and sentiments that together gradually shape or mold the sort of person we become and are eventually known to be. Far from simply regulating outward behavior and appearance, mores describe the set of influences that contribute to the form or character of the soul of any given individual or nation.

Whereas Lincoln drew upon an understanding of modern republicanism based on natural rights that had been developed by the "state of nature" philosophers of the 17th and 18th centuries and which had provided the principled basis for both the American and French revolutions (mediated especially by John Locke in the American case and by Jean-Jacques Rousseau in France), Tocqueville was acutely aware (both politically and personally) of the way in which the principles of natural right were used to justify the reign of terror in the aftermath of the French revolution. Rather than embracing the philosophic form of modern republicanism that had originated with Hobbes and was powerfully developed by Locke (among others)— one that ascribed inalienable and universal rights to pre-political individuals living in a hypothetical "state of nature"—Tocqueville was

much more drawn to the tradition of modern republicanism inaugu-
rated by Montesquieu and developed by Edmund Burke. James Ceaser has described the foundation for this latter tradition as "customary
history"; it is characterized by sensitivity to and awareness of the powerfully formative influence of the particular and idiosyncratic facts
that provide the ongoing and always-developing historical and political contexts in which all human beings find themselves.[7]

The Problematic Character of Abstract Ideas

What then is problematic about guiding or shaping republican politics in accordance with abstract principles discovered by philosophic
reason? The core problem is suggested by the very word used by Lincoln to praise Jefferson's singular achievement in writing the Declaration of Independence: by definition, universal principles "abstract"
from the particular historical or political contexts from which they
emerge. Whereas one might be tempted to think that abstract principles always mean the same thing, this is not entirely true in politics
since the meaning of those principles depends on how they are understood by those who affirm them. The way in which one understands
an abstract principle is deeply influenced by the particular "mores"
that invariably shape both the heart and mind of any given human
being or any given people. The fundamental principles of liberty and
equality in fact mean different things in different historical and political contexts because of the powerful influence of mores in shaping the
way we perceive those principles—both for good and for ill.

For example, the inalienable right to liberty affirmed by the
Declaration of Independence is often understood and used in contemporary American society to defend the right of individuals to grat-
ify as many desires as they wish, provided only that these actions do
not infringe upon the rights of others. Whereas most exercise their

---

[7] James W. Ceaser, "Alexis de Tocqueville and the Two-Founding Thesis,"
in *The Review of Politics* 73 (2011): 219-243. See also Ceaser's *Nature and History
in American Political Development*, (Cambridge MA and London: Harvard University Press, 2006).

liberty to pursue the accumulation of wealth, some choose to practice public philanthropy, while others invoke their publically sanctioned freedom to enjoy the pleasures of sex among consenting adults. In sharp contrast to this last example (the official philosophy of the once-popular Playboy magazine), liberty can also be understood as both a form and result of sustained self-discipline; by slowly developing one's capacity to exercise self-control or moderation, human beings are able to liberate themselves from the tyranny of the passions.

I have drawn the last two contrasting conceptions of liberty from part of Tocqueville's account of America's first Puritan founding. Reflecting on a famous speech by John Winthrop, Tocqueville maintains that license and liberty are in fact two different things. Winthrop distinguishes the liberty of human beings "to do what they list" (license), from what he considers to be a genuine "liberty for the just and good," (something that presupposes self-rule) (1.1.2, 42). Notwithstanding this traditional distinction between license and liberty made by Winthrop and praised by Tocqueville, both can and have been justified by invoking the same inalienable right to liberty. The particular understanding of liberty that prevails at any given historical moment will always reflect a specific web of shared customs, practices, ideas, beliefs, and sentiments—which is to say, the distinctive historical and cultural mores of those who are effectively interpreting or giving meaning and content to the abstract principle in question.

A second highly relevant example has been the remarkable shift in the American understanding of individual rights in the years since they were first posited in the Declaration of Independence. As initially articulated by Locke and affirmed by the signers of the Declaration of Independence, the invocation of equal rights to life, liberty and the pursuit of happiness were meant to limit the reach of government into the private lives of citizens by guaranteeing to all equal treatment before the law, freedom of worship, free elections, and economic opportunity. However, socially-conscious reformers in the first half of the 20th century argued that individual freedom could only be realized if the government guaranteed an additional set of "economic rights," including the right to housing, medical care, and protection against the economic fears of old age, sickness, accidents, and unemployment.[8] In the aftermath of the 1960's, the language of rights was further extended to include gay rights, abortion rights, the right to privacy, and the rights of criminal defendants. And in the 21st century we are using the language of rights to change the meaning of marriage and put the national government in charge of health insurance.

Whether one regrets or applauds these developments, the point I wish to make is that Americans were never more dependent upon government, and that government was never so intimately involved in the specific details of individual lives as it is today. Paradoxically, what originally began as an invocation of universal principles intended to promote individual freedom by limiting the power of government, has since been used to justify an immense governmental expansion; and what was originally intended to guarantee individual independence has inadvertently brought into being a culture of dependence usually described under the rubric of "the welfare state." Not only do individual rights mean something dramatically different today than they did in 1776, but contemporary invocations of rights are typically claims that government provide citizens with a growing array of services, rather than an insistence that government limit itself so that citizens are free to provide for themselves.

It would be unfair, even absurd, to attribute all these developments to the "abstract truths" affirmed in the Declaration of Independence. Rather, my point is to clarify the underlying reason for Tocqueville's unwillingness to embrace an understanding of modern republicanism grounded in abstract principles of right, and to begin to explain the surprising absence of any consideration of the Declaration of Independence in his study of American democracy.[9] The core

---

[8] See FDR's Commonwealth Club Campaign speech in 1932, and his State of the Union Address on January 11, 1944. My articulation of the shift to a more expansive understanding of individual rights was influenced by "20th Century Revolutions: The Expansion of Freedom" at www.digitalhistory.UH.edu.

[9] Tocqueville's failure to recognize or even mention the principles articulated in the Declaration of Independence was initially brought into public view and pointedly criticized by Thomas G. West in "Misunderstanding the American

problem is that reliance on universal principles—precisely because they abstract from the specific historical and cultural mores in which they are embedded—can lead to the paradoxical situation I have just described, one in which the same universal principle of liberty can be used to justify the replacement of an earlier understanding with a new one that is diametrically opposed to important aspects of the intent or aim of the original affirmation.

Tocqueville, Lincoln and Modern Political Philosophy

At the top of the list of those who by inclination, education or occupation are drawn to abstract ideas or general principles, Tocqueville places philosophers—and especially those who came into the forefront of politics during the Enlightenment.[10] Philosophers of all times and places are especially attracted to abstract, universal or general principles by virtue of their clarity, consistency, explanatory power, and replicability. These are in fact the characteristics of reason itself, the "sole compass and guiding star" of the philosophic life (to use Locke's phrase), and the authoritative principle by which science—ancient or modern—is guided. The "state of nature" theorists of the 17th and 18th centuries—most notably Hobbes, Locke and Rousseau—all sought to make general, indeed universal, inferences about human nature. Notwithstanding deep differences, all three described

Founding," in *Interpreting Tocqueville's Democracy in America,* edited by Ken Masugi (Savage, MD: Rowman & Littlefield, 1991) 155-177.

[10] In Tocqueville's speech to the *Academy of Moral and Political Sciences* in 1852, he indicates both the importance and limitations of political philosophy and the science of politics. He also points out that great political writers are often captivated by the logic of ideas and develop a taste for the subtle, ingenious and original in a way that renders them especially ill-suited for the practice of politics. This is because political practice is more often moved by passion rather than logic and by simplified opinions rather than subtle argumentation. This speech was translated and published in English for the first time as "The Art & Science of Politics: An Unpublished Speech" by J. P. Mayer in *Encounter* 26 (1971): 27-35. A new translation by Joseph L. Hebert appears in *Alexis de Tocqueville and the Art of Democratic Statesmanship,* edited by Brian Danoff and L. Joseph Hebert (Lanham, MD: Rowman & Littlefield, 2011) 17-29.

a pre-political "state of nature" in which individuals were both free and equal. In Rousseau's image, just as one might try to scrape accretions and barnacles from an ancient statue retrieved from a sunken ship so as to view something of its original condition, the state of nature philosophers sought to display human nature in its pristine form—that is, they attempted to supply their readers with an image of human nature as it first emerged from the hands of "Nature or Nature's God," as Jefferson expressed it in the Declaration of Independence. Their common goal was to provide a truly universal ground or starting point for the study and practice of politics, one that could function as an alternative to the theologically contested and politically problematic teachings of Biblical religion. Hobbes, Locke and Rousseau, notwithstanding their very real differences, all sought to find "another rise of government," to use Locke's characteristically understated phrase, one that took its bearings from a more scientific understanding of human nature based on human reason rather than from the contested and often non-verifiable claims emanating from competing versions of Christianity.[11]

Whereas Tocqueville's acute awareness of the dangers of abstract philosophical principles in politics leads him to omit any reference to the Declaration of Independence in his study of America, Lincoln bases his statecraft on precisely those principles, brilliantly utilizing them both to preserve the Union and to bring an end to America's most flagrant violation of its own publicly-stated self-understanding. Lincoln's reliance on the second paragraph of the Declaration of Independence bespeaks an initial indebtedness to the natural rights theory of government and therefore indirectly to the "state of nature" theorists of the 17th and 18th centuries from which it was drawn. However, in the course of affirming the importance of this document, Lincoln also modifies its meaning in a way that departs from the philosophic understanding from which it first arose. Whereas

---

[11] In the 18th century the study of morality, politics and political philosophy were considered sciences. Writing in the 19th century Tocqueville calls for "a new science of politics," one that he presumably exhibits in his published books.

Hobbes, Locke and Rousseau had described a free and equal pre-political "state of nature," Lincoln took the inherent equality and liberty ascribed to an original human condition and made it the positive aspirational goal and noble work of the American republic itself. The self-evident natural rights of the Declaration of Independence which had served as the fundamental standard for legitimate government during the founding period, became under Lincoln's leadership during the crisis of civil war,

> a standard maxim for free society, which should be familiar to all, and revered by all; constantly looked to, constantly labored for, and even though never perfectly attained, constantly approximated, and thereby constantly spreading and deepening its influence and augmenting the happiness and value of life *to all people of all colors everywhere* (emphasis added).[12]

For Lincoln, commitment to this effort constituted the particular shared purpose of the American republic (although for Lincoln, like Jefferson, it need by no means be limited to the American republic). If the Constitution cleverly exploits the principle of self-interest to bolster the security and stability of those who agree to live under its authority, Lincoln found in the abstract truths of the Declaration of Independence the particular form of justice by which Americans could be encouraged to look beyond their immediate interests and toward a truly common good. What is more, the always-unfinished character of this work insures that the noble purpose of the American republic can, at least in principle, persist into an indefinite future.[13]

---

[12] This is taken from Lincoln's "Speech on the Dred Scott Decision," July 26, 1857 in *Writings*, 108-119, esp. 115.

[13] Unlike the Progressive movement which emerged in America during the first half of the 20th century alluded to earlier in this essay, Lincoln's designation of the always-unfinished aspiration of modern republicanism is grounded in awareness of a fundamental or permanent problem. That is, he does not set forth a progressive agenda to be fully realized in the future, but gives expression to his own awareness of the limits of political justice at all times and places. It is precisely because fallible human beings are incapable of enacting and sustaining *perfect political justice*, that the noble work of spreading, deepening and augmenting political justice will never be fully implemented or exhausted. If this insistence on

In sharp contrast to Tocqueville, Lincoln was able to utilize abstract truths grounded in Enlightenment philosophy not only to preserve a divided nation, but also as a weapon against the powerful pull of political indifference on the slavery question. Lincoln characterizes Stephen Douglas' appeal to state sovereignty on the slavery issue as a "declared indifference." It is an indifference that Lincoln says he,

> can not but hate...because of the monstrous injustice of slavery itself,...because it deprives [the American] republican example of its just influence in the world,...and especially because it forces so many really good men...into an open war with the very fundamental principles of civil liberty [by] criticizing the Declaration of Independence, and insisting that there is no right principle of action but *self-interest* (emphasis in original).[14]

Without his appeal to and insistence upon universal principle, it is hard to imagine that Lincoln could have succeeded in preserving the Union and abolishing slavery, what he refers to in his Second Inaugural Address as the unlooked for but "fundamental and astounding" result of a war that had exceeded in cost, suffering and duration the expectations of either side. Lincoln however, did more than preserve the Union; by ending its most fundamental congenital inconsistency, he also directed the American republic to a higher purpose, one that made it *worth* preserving.

Principles or Mores?

Unlike Lincoln, Tocqueville's extended study of and reflection on the problem of slavery in America led him to confess that he could find no way through the American impasse (1.2.10). Should we then put Lincoln on the side of the philosophers criticized by Tocqueville, those whose dangerous abstractions Tocqueville subordinates to the

---

the limits of justice seems depressing to some, its corollary is not: there will always be good, important, and challenging work to be done.

[14] This is from Lincoln's speech on the Kansas-Nebraska Act in his first debate with Senator Douglas in Peoria, Illinois, October 16, 1854 in *Writings*, 66.

importance of historically developed and embedded mores? Although I have begun to sketch a substantial difference between Lincoln and Tocqueville concerning their respective understandings of the proper ground or foundation for modern republicanism—philosophic principle or the cultivation of mores—there are also reasons to believe that their different approaches to and understandings of modern republican politics are in fact closer than would initially appear to be the case.

First, in turning to the abstract principles of the Declaration of Independence, Lincoln was *not* turning in any explicit way to the doctrines of the Enlightenment philosophers, but was taking his bearings from the distinctive political history of the American republic. Far from introducing the kind of philosophic or "literary politics" condemned by Tocqueville in his analysis of the French revolution, Lincoln looked to an important, authoritative and uniquely American document. Indeed, Jefferson insisted that in writing the Declaration, he had not written anything original, but was attempting to provide "an expression of the American mind, and give to that expression the proper tone and spirit called for by the occasion." He goes on to explain that "all of its [the Declaration's] authority" rests on having succeeded in "harmonizing the sentiments of the day" (Letter to Henry Lee, May 8, 1825). Lincoln understood himself to be drawing upon deeply held beliefs and sentiments that had characterized the American people since the inception of the nation, despite the fact that they were only inconsistently adhered to and even egregiously violated in practice.

If Lincoln was drawing upon the best and most authoritative expression of the mores of the American people, Tocqueville was not entirely unaware of the importance of principle in politics. He too insists on the importance of universal rights that inhere in each individual, but traces their origin and foundation to an event that predates not only the Enlightenment but the American experience altogether. Tocqueville famously writes, "[I]t was necessary for Jesus Christ to come to earth to make it understood that all members of the human species are naturally alike and equal" (2.1.3, 413). Although it may be true that the modern world finds itself alienated from Christianity's core *theological* beliefs, Tocqueville maintains that it remains profoundly indebted to Christianity for its most pervasive *ethical* convictions. Indeed, for Tocqueville, it was not modern philosophy, nor was it the French or American revolutions that provided the original impetus for the sweeping democratic revolution that he chronicles in the Introduction to his book; it was rather Christianity.[15] It is not that Tocqueville fails to see anything new in modern democratic politics, but that, "almost all that we call modern principles should be considered as new consequences drawn from the old Christian principles."[16]

Tocqueville, like Lincoln, emphasizes the importance of individual rights, but by pointing to the Biblical (rather than modern philosophic) source for those rights. In so doing, he draws upon a specific religious context that explicitly recognizes—indeed insists—that these rights are accompanied by duties and responsibilities. In fact, Tocqueville believed that the persistence of this Christian context in America had enabled Americans to avoid—at least so far—the dangerous drift toward "individualism." By individualism Tocqueville means the modern democratic tendency to withdraw from the larger society of which one is a part into a small circle of family and friends. In addition to political apathy, individualism in America tends to take the form of restless and often excessive preoccupation with private material well-being, which, according to Tocqueville, eventually impedes or contracts the full development of the human soul (2.2.2). Indeed, he looks upon individualism as a potentially fatal weakness in modern democracy that, in the American case, explicitly deploys the

---

[15] It is telling that Tocqueville describes the democratic revolution taking place "in all the *Christian* universe" (emphasis added) (DA Introduction, p. 6). For an explanation and assessment of Tocqueville's thesis on the Christian origin of the democratic revolution, see Aristide Tessitore, "Tocqueville and Gobineau on the Nature of Modern Politics," in *The Review of Politics* Vol. 67 No. 4 (Fall 2005): 631-657.

[16] This quotation is taken from Tocqueville's correspondence with Arthur de Gobineau in 1843, edited and translated by John Lukacs in *The European Revolution and Correspondence with Gobineau* (Garden City NY: Doubleday Anchor, 1958) 211; cf. 192-94, 207.

self-interested character of the human soul to advance the shared political goods of security and prosperity.

Tocqueville is of course fully aware of the ineradicable character of self-interest in the human soul and even acknowledges that the Enlightenment principle of self-interest well understood is of all philosophic doctrines, the one most appropriate for our own time (1.2.6, 227-9). However, in *Democracy in America* he consistently points to the value, importance and usefulness of Biblical religion as a needed counterweight to the inescapable pull of self-interest in human affairs. Notwithstanding the hierarchical structure of the Christian Middle Ages, Tocqueville emphasizes the essential compatibility between Christianity and democratic principles as long as religion remains in its own proper sphere—which is not politics, but the family. Paradoxically, it is the *indirect* influence of religion on politics, based on its capacity to shape the hearts and minds of individuals and its power to mold the moral sensibilities of the young, which leads Tocqueville to call religion "the first of America's political institutions" (1.2.9, 278-82).

In sum, Lincoln was drawing upon the "mores" of the American people in the way in which Tocqueville understood and used that word; and Tocqueville was not entirely averse to or unaware of the importance and usefulness of principle in politics—even philosophically generated ones—provided that they are accompanied by a concern for and attentiveness to those habits of heart and mind that determine how those principles are understood and interpreted.

Political Experience or Rational Design?

If the different weight assigned to principle and mores in the thought of Lincoln and Tocqueville does not entirely preclude some common ground, the extent and limits of reason in politics reveals a second important area of agreement, one that also informs their respective understandings of modern republicanism. In his assessment of the powerful influence of 18th century philosophy on the French revolution, Tocqueville is sharply critical of the misplaced, even if well-intentioned, belief that it is possible to clean up the messiness of political practice by reducing politics to purely rational principles drawn from reason alone. Tocqueville's study of the French revolution leads him to conclude that despite the different and even irreconcilable character of the "abstract and literary" political teachings that took the lead in France during the revolution, all agreed on a single general idea that provided them with common ground and a shared goal. All thought it a good idea "to substitute basic and simple principles derived from reason and natural law, for the complicated and traditional customs which ruled the society of their times" (ORR, 196).[17] Although the idea was hardly new (consider Aristotle's critique of attempts to impose an abstract rational order on politics by Phaleus and Hippodamus in the *Politics* 2.7-8), what was new was the way in which this idea managed to seize the minds of almost all writers during this period, making it, according to Tocqueville, the core principle of "the political philosophy of the eighteenth century" (ORR, 196).

Tocqueville explains that the sight of so many "abusive and ridiculous privileges" drew socially-minded writers and reformers to the idea of a natural equality among the ranks, and that the sight of bizarre and irregular institutions that had outlived their original context readily filled philosophers with "a disgust for old things and for tradition." The result was as understandable as it was unfortunate. Philosophers and those influenced by them were naturally led to a desire to rebuild contemporary society "according to an entirely new plan, that each of them drew from the inspiration of his reason alone" (ORR, 196-7). Their complete lack of political experience, however, left them completely bereft of any awareness of "the dangers that invariably accompany even the most necessary revolutions" (ORR, 197). Indeed, they were completely blind to the fact that their shared desire for "a simultaneous and systematic abolition of all the laws and all the

---

[17] Citations from Tocqueville's *The Old Regime and the Revolution* refer to the edition edited by François Furet and Françoise Mélonio and translated by Alan S. Kahan (Chicago and London: University of Chicago Press, 1998).

customs in use in the country" would amount to a vast, violent and dangerous revolution (ORR, 199).

This kind of abstract and naïve desire to sweep away in a single bold stroke the slow evolution of customs and traditions over centuries without any appreciation for the importance of the mores they nurtured and sustained, or of the violence and political chaos it was bound to release, is about as foreign to Lincoln's way of thinking about the possibilities and limitations of reason in politics as one could imagine. In the measure that Lincoln brought philosophic intelligence to bear upon his understanding and practice of politics, it was characterized by keen awareness of the limits of politics and especially the limited extent to which politics could be organized or informed by principles drawn from reason alone.[18] In this respect, Lincoln's understanding of politics has much more in common with Aristotle or even Tocqueville himself, than it does with the 18th century Enlightenment philosophers and their precursors. It is certainly true that a good measure of Lincoln's greatness as a statesman is revealed by his ability to articulate the overarching principles and aims that animate his particular political decisions and policies. This ability, however, was unfailingly accompanied by another, namely his capacity to make the kind of political compromises necessary to keep open the possibility that those principles might be more fully implemented at some point in the future. For example, Lincoln consistently maintained that slavery was both evil in itself and corrosive to modern republican government, while guaranteeing that he would protect slavery in those states where it already existed. He also insisted that the Dred Scott decision was a perverse reading of the Constitution

---

[18] Early in his political career Lincoln wrote: "Passion...will in future be our enemy. Reason, cold, calculating, unimpassioned reason, must furnish all the materials for our future support and defense." However, that same speech called for "every American to pledge his life, his liberty, and his sacred honor" to "support the Constitution and Laws" even to the point of "veneration," such that the achievement of the founding generation might "become the *political religion* of the nation" (emphasis in original) (Address to the Young Man's Lyceum of Springfield, January 27, 1838) in *Writings* esp. 14, 11.

and used his position and considerable rhetorical abilities to keep its problematic character before the public eye, all the while dutifully enforcing the fugitive slave law because it had been sanctioned (albeit indirectly) by the Constitution.[19] Unlike the philosophers and physiocrats whose literary politics animated the French revolution, Lincoln was well acquainted with the particular idiosyncrasies of American politics and was under no illusion that politics could be made to conform to principles drawn from reason alone. In sum, Lincoln was adept at making the kind of compromises that are the price of progress in politics, and, perhaps most remarkably, he was able to do so in a way that kept fully visible the overarching principles that gave meaning and dignity to his policies.

Conclusion

Tocqueville and Lincoln profoundly differed in their understanding of the foundations of the American republic. Although both looked to and admired the Constitution, neither thought that its ingenious deployment of "wholly new discoveries" in political science—those that enabled it to channel, and even harness, the darker passions of the human heart (see *Federalist* 9,10 and 51)—could adequately account for crucial aspects of American political practice, especially for the more generous behaviors exhibited by the American people. Whereas Lincoln found America's core beliefs and noblest aspirations best expressed in the ringing affirmation of equality and liberty inserted into American history by the foresight of the author of the Declaration of Independence, Tocqueville's overriding preoccupation with mores led him to trace the remote first cause of those same principles to the revolution in thought inspired by Christianity and brought to America 150 years earlier by the Christian and especially Puritan "first founders." Whereas Lincoln effectively uses the universal prin-

---

[19] Allen Guelzo argues that for Lincoln, "the Constitution, rightly read in its original context, gave only provisional sanction to slavery." See "Did Lincoln Kill the Constitution?" by Allen C. Guelzo, The Witherspoon Fellowship Lectures, October 21, 1999. See esp. 5-6.

ciples of the Declaration of Independence to preserve the Union, abolish slavery, and call Americans to the noble work of extending the equal right of liberty to all, Tocqueville emphasizes the need to attend to mores and, notwithstanding the anti-religious inclinations of modern philosophy and educated European opinion, he encourages readers to deepen their appreciation for the ennobling aspects of their religious inheritance.

Despite deep differences in their understanding of the foundation of modern republicanism, I have also sought to bring to light a substantial overlap in their understanding of the nature and limits inherent in politics. Had Tocqueville lived long enough to witness Lincoln's leadership through the tragedy of civil war, it is hard to imagine that he would not admire America's 16th President, despite inevitable differences of opinion about some matters. It is likewise hard to imagine that Lincoln's own effort to preserve America's experiment in self-government would not welcome Tocqueville's insight into the democratic soul in general, and the spotlight he shines on mores in particular. The most appropriate conclusion to be drawn from this comparison of Tocqueville and Lincoln is not, I think, the superiority of one perspective over the other, but deeper awareness of the usefulness of both philosophic principle and mores—even or perhaps especially religious mores—for nurturing and sustaining healthy political life.[20]

Modern democratic republics face a number of serious external challenges at the beginning of the 21st century. But perhaps none are as urgent or consequential as those that arise from within, whether it be the incremental and self-enacted disappearance of the nation-state in Europe or the slide toward individualism and ever-expanding

---

[20] As we have noted, Lincoln originally encouraged a type of political religion in his Address at the Young Man's Lyceum in 1838. However, after presiding over a war that far exceeded anything anticipated by either side, he turns to a general version of America's longstanding and culturally embedded engagement with Biblical religion in his Second Inaugural Address in 1865, as he tries to make sense of the catastrophic loss and suffering of civil war, as well as its "fundamental and astounding" result (*Writings*, 428-429).

growth of the administrative state in America. In both cases, modern republics need to find ways to extend the benefits of unprecedented prosperity without, however, a corresponding loss in genuine political freedom. The freedom in question depends upon cultivating citizens who are willing and able to undertake the responsibility of governing themselves. If the now longstanding success of the American experiment with modern republicanism is to endure, there is still much to be learned from the political wisdom of both Tocqueville and Lincoln as we confront new challenges to both individual and political freedom in the increasingly global and democratic future that looms before us.

INDEX